ISCHIA
THE ISLAND OF THE SPRINGS

PROCIDA-POZZUOLI-BACOLI
CAPO MISENO-BAIA-CUMA

BONECHI

Publication created and designed by *Casa Editrice Bonechi*
Publication manager: *Monica Bonechi*
Picture research, graphic design and cover: *Sonia Gottardo*
Video make-up: *Bernardo Dionisio*
Text: *Patrizia Fabbri*
Editing: *Simonetta Giorgi*
Translation: *Julia Weiss*
Map: *Studio Grafico Daniela Mariani, Pistoia*

© Copyright by Casa Editrice Bonechi - Firenze - Italia
e-mail: bonechi@bonechi.it - Internet: www.bonechi.it

Printed in Italy by
Centro Stampa Editoriale Bonechi - Sesto Fiorentino

The photos from the archives of *Casa Editrice Bonechi* are by *Paolo Giambone, MSA* and *Foto Castello*.

Contributing Photographers:
Massimo Amendola (pages 33 bottom right and left, 61 bottom left, 74 bottom left);
Gaetano Barone (pages 6, 26-27, 35-36, 61 top, 73 top and bottom, 93, 98 top);
Andrea Pistolesi (pages 4, 5, 10 bottom left, 11, 13 top and center, 14, 15 top and center, 16 top left,
17 center and bottom right and left, 19 top and bottom, 20 center, 21 top and right in the box,
23, 32, 33 top right and center, 40-45, 47, 49, 50 top left and bottom, 52-53, 58-60, 64 top, 65-66, 67 top,
68, 70, 71 bottom, 74 top and bottom right, 77, 81-82, 84, 85 bottom right and left, 86 bottom right and left,
87, 88 top right and left, 90, 91 top left and bottom);
Ghigo Roli (pages 31, 61 bottom right in the box, 62 top, 63 top left and bottom, 67 bottom,
75, 91 top right in the box, 92, 95 top, 99).

Photos pages 7, 73 center courtesy of *Azienda Autonoma di Cura, Soggiorno e Turismo
delle Isole di Ischia e Procida.*

Photos page 51 top right, center, and bottom right and left courtesy of *Maria Fiore Batini.*

ISBN 88-476-0727-2

INTRODUCTION

The earliest recorded name of Ischia was *Arime*, which is what Homer called it. The Roman poets of the Augustan era called it *Inarime*, while others used *Aenaria*. The current name seems to derive from the Latin *insula*, for island. The natural changes that have taken place on the island of Ischia over the course of the centuries were much more numerous than its changes of name. The history of what is also known as "the green island" is marked by earthquakes and eruptions. Ischia is the visible part of a volcanic field that comprises Monte Epomeo (788 meters) that still takes up much of its land today and many eruptive centers that are not always recognizable because they have been destroyed or covered by long series of eruptions. Recent geological studies have made it possible to draw an accurate chronological map of the island's volcanic activities. They began more than 130,000 years ago, alternating periods of quiescence and great turbulence until the historical era, with enormous repercussions on the island's morphology and life in general. Many archeological finds confirm human presence in the area overlooking what is now the town of Lacco Ameno dating back to the Bronze Age. Pottery shards from the Mycenaean age, datable between the XV and XIV centuries BC have been found on the coastal strip between Ischia Porto and Casamicciola, specifically on the Castiglione hill. During the first half of the VIII century BC Euboic, Chalcidian and Eretrian settlers came to an area northeast of Monte Vico. At the base of the promontory two natural harbors favored sailing and trade of the new colony. Its name, *Pithecusa*, was later extended to the whole island. This name has two probable origins: either *pythos* a clay jar, because of the flourishing local pottery industry, or *pithekos* that means monkey, after its mythical inhabitants, the Cercopes that Hercules transformed into monkeys. The ships brought the island its fortunes. Following a violent eruption at the end of the VI century BC, the Chalcidians and Eretrians abandoned the area. In 474 BC the island facing the coast at the height of what is now Ischia Ponte, was occupied by Gerone di Siracusa who built a military fort that was known as Castel Gerone in the Middle Ages. A few years later another eruption forced the inhabitants of the fort to abandon the island that was later occupied by the Romans drawn there by the hot springs and healthy climate; the only drawbacks were the constant volcanic and seismic events. The early centuries of the Christian era were not distinguished by any particular events except for the Saracen invasion during the IX century. They devastated the inhabited areas and plundered the islanders. Later, some areas were selected for rural and religious settlements. Around the year 1000, for example, a Basilian monastery was established over the ruins of an ancient settlement in the east near the Promontorio di San Pietro. Other, Augustinian monasteries date from the XII century. The terrible eruption of 1301 forced the island to be temporarily abandoned: its inhabitants found refuge on Baia and Capri, and returned four years later, to settle at the Isolotto del Castello. From the Anjou era to the end of the XVI century the area was densely repopulated, thanks mainly to the guarantee of safety that the location offered. The life of the islanders, however, was to be influenced by the tumultuous events of the Kingdom of Naples, and times were particularly hard during the turbulent period of the Anjou-Durazzo struggles. In 1422 Giovanna II gave Ischia to her adopted son Alfonso of Aragon, who in 1438 linked his name to an event that was as incredible as it was unusual. He banished all the males from the island and established a colony of Catalans who were quickly married to the wives and daughters of the exiles. Then in 1442 Alfonso gave the Ischian castle to his mistress Lucrezia d'Alagno, it then passed to the Torellas who were banished from the island by Ferdinando I. Ferdinando II sought refuge on the island following the advent of Carlo VIII and in 1495 killed the castellan and imposed the rule of Innico d'Avalos whose family continued to rule the entire area until the eighteenth century. In 1729 when the D'Avalos dynasty died out, the island became a *universitas* or university and was entrusted to the state, just for a short time however, because in 1734 it came under Bourbon rule. In 1799 Admiral Nelson quelled the tumults that had exploded throughout the island that wanted its independence. But on 13 February 1809 Ischia was occupied by the French who on 24 June overcame the last bit of resistance by the English who were barricaded in the castle This date was to be particularly tragic because Murat's troops wreaked incredible devastation leaving a profound mark on the life, art and history of the whole island. Part of the fortifications, the beautiful cathedral and other buildings were almost entirely razed to the ground. Today, travelers arriving at Ischia dock at the port of the same name, the island's most important harbor. This is an island with a natural environment, crystalline waters and the universally acknowledged therapeutic effects of its hot springs and mud, that has given it a charm that is now its main economic resource.

THE THERMAL WATERS

THE SPRINGS AT BARANO

GIARDINI OLIMPUS - Spiaggia Maronti tel.081 990032
HELIOS TERME - Via Maronti tel. 081 900001
LA MANDORLA - Spiaggia Maronti tel. 081 990046
PARCO SMERALDO - Spiaggia Maronti tel. 081 990127
SAN RAPHAEL TERME - Testaccio tel. 081 980508
TERME DI NITRODI - tel. 081 990064

THE SPRINGS AT CASAMICCIOLA

CRISTALLO PALACE - Via Eddomade tel. 081 994362
LA PERGOLA - Via Casa Mennella tel. 081 994902
IBSEN - Via V. Emanuele, 35 tel. 081 994588
MIRAMONTI E MARE - Viale Paradisiello tel. 081 994600
PARCO TERMALE CASTIGLIONE - SS. 270 tel. 081 982551
STEFANIA - Piazzetta Nizzola tel. 081 994130
STELLA MARIS - Via S. Girardi tel. 081 994440
TERME BELLIAZZI - Piazza Bagni tel. 081 994580
TERME ELISABETTA - Via Garibaldi tel. 081 994355
TERME ELMA - Via V. Emanuele tel. 081 994919
TERME FIOLA - Via Ombrasco tel. 081 994502
TERME LUCIBELLO - Via Garibaldi tel. 081 994420
TERME MALTEMPO - Via Garibaldi tel. 081 994540
TERME MANZI - Piazza Bagni tel. 081 994722
TERME RITA 1 - Via La Rita tel. 081 995484
TERME RITA 2 - Via La Rita tel. 081 994242
TERME RITA F. MONTI - Via S. Antonio tel. 081 995064
TERME ROSALEO - tel. 081 994681
TERME VERDE - Piazzetta Nizzola tel. 081 994500
TUSCULUM - tel. 081 994265
VINETUM - Via D'Aloysio tel. 081 994290

THE SPRINGS AT FORIO

GIARDINI POSEIDON - Spiaggia Citara tel. 081 907122
IL GATTOPARDO - tel. 081 997714
PARCO MARIA - Cuotto tel. 081 907322
PARK IMPERIAL - SS. 270, Località Cuotto tel. 081 907170
PUNTA DEL SOLE - Via G. Maltese tel. 081 990208
ROYAL PALM - tel. 081 907198
SAN NICOLA - SS. 270 tel. 081 907247
STUFE DI SAN LORENZO - SS. 270, Loc. Lacco Ameno
  tel. 081 994115
TERME CASTALDI - Via Montenerone tel. 081 997101
TERME COIELLA - Via Montenerone tel. 081 997035
TRAMONTO D'ORO - SS. 270 (Forio Panza) tel. 081 997963
TRITONE - Via Cesotta tel. 081 987471
VILLA ANGELA - SS. 270 (Forio Panza) tel. 081 997648
VILLA THOMAS TERME - Via Montenerone tel. 081 997340

THE SPRINGS AT ISCHIA

AMBASCIATORI - Via E. Gianturco tel. 081 992933
ANTONELLA - Via Morgioni, 42 tel. 081 993566
ARAGONA PALACE - Via Porto tel. 081 981401

BRISTOL - tel. 081 992181
CENTRAL PARK - Via A. de Luca tel. 081 993517
CONTINENTAL TERME - Via M. Mazzella tel. 081 991588
DELLE TERME JOLLY - Via A. de Luca tel. 081 991744
EXCELSIOR - Via E. Gianturco, 3 tel. 081 991522
FIORIDIANA - Corso V. Colonna, 16 tel. 081 981014
HERMITAGE E PARK - Via L. Mazzella tel. 081 992395
IL MORESCO - Via E. Gianturco, 16 tel. 081 981355
ISCHIA THERMAL BOTTOM - Via delle Terme tel. 081 984376
LA VILIAROSA - Via G. Gigante tel. 081 991316
LETIZIA - Via L. Mazzella tel. 081 992080
MARE BLU - Via Pontano, 40 tel. 081 982938
ORIENTE - Via delle Terme, 9/11 tel. 081 991306
PARCO AURORA - Via F. D'Avalos tel. 081 982022
PARCO EDERA - Via Morgioni tel. 081 993046
PARCO EDERA - Via Morgioni, 28 tel. 081 991313
PARCO VERDE - Via M. Mazzella tel. 081 992282
PRESIDENT - Circumval. Ischia tel. 081 993890
PUNTA MOLINO - Via Champault tel. 081 991544
REGINA PALACE - Via E. Cortese, 18 tel. 081 991344
SAN GIOVANNI - Via E. Sogliuzzo tel. 081 991122
SANVALENTINO - Via L. Mazzella tel. 081 982088
SOLEMAR - Via Battistessa, 45 tel. 081 991822
STAB. BALNEO TERMALE MILITARE - Antica Reggia tel. 081 991008
STRAND DELFINI - Via N. Cartaromana, 54 tel. 081 981341
TERME ALEXANDER - Lungomare C. Colombo tel. 081 993409
TERME FELIX - Via A. de Luca tel. 081 991201
TERME ROYAL - Via delle Terme tel. 081 991002

THE SPRINGS AT LACCO AMENO

AUGUSTO TERME - Via del Campo tel. 081 994944
DON PEPE - Via Circumvallazione tel. 081 994397
EUROPEO CLUB - Corso Angelo Rizzoli tel. 081 994384
GRAZIA - Via Fango tel. 081 994333
LA PACE TERME - Via Oneso tel. 081 994305
LA REGINELLA - Piazza Santa Restituta tel. 081 994300
MICHELANGELO - Via Fango tel. 081 995134
PARCO NEGOMBO - Spiaggia San Montano tel. 081 986152
PRINCIPE - Via del Campo tel. 081 994466
SAN MONTANO - tel. 081 994033
TERME MARINA - Corso Angelo Rizzoli tel. 081 994503
TERME REGINA ISABELLA - Piazza Santa Restituta tel. 081 994223
VILLA SVIZZERA - Via Litoranea tel. 081 994263

THE SPRINGS AT SERRARA

CAVA SCURA - Maronti tel. 081 905564
GIARDINI DI APHRODITE - Via Fondolillo tel. 081 999202
GIARDINI DI APOLLON - Via Fondolillo tel. 081 999272
GIARDINO TROPICAL - Via Chiaia delle Rose tel. 081 999242
LA PALMA - tel. 081 999215
ROMANTICA TERME - Via Cava Ruffano tel. 081 999216
TERME CASA ROSA - Via Fondolillo tel. 081 999328
TERME LINDA (HOTEL MIRAMARE) - Via Fondolillo tel. 081 999219
TERME SAN MICHELE - Via Sant'Angelo tel. 081 999276
TERME VULCANO - Via Fondolillo tel. 081 999322

THE ISLAND OF THE SPRINGS

In a splendid environmental setting, Ischia offers fully equipped spa facilities for a particularly delightful stay.

Ischia, with its nearly 50 square kilometers of area and unmistakable trapezoidal shape is the largest of the Neapolitan islands, situated between Procida and Capri, about 30 km from the mainland. The island is rich in thermal waters that spring from the ground and sea nearly everywhere as proof of its volcanic origins. Ever since the time of the ancient Greek settlements, these waters have been the island's peculiar treasure. The springs of different temperatures offer a wide range of therapeutic applications, some of which have not changed over the course of millennia. Even though Pliny and Strabo had on more than one occasion lauded the effectiveness of Ischia's springs that enjoyed a moment of glory during the Imperial Roman era, it was not until much later, in the XVII century, with the medical-scientific study of the organoleptic and curative properties of the waters, that Ischia was able to embark on a path on which it was to remain forever. Actually, in the sixteenth century Giulio Iasolino rediscovered the springs at Casamicciola and brought the "spa" industry to a decisive reawakening. Even before him, in the XIV century, Giovanni da Casamicciola, personal physician to Charles of Anjou had superficially studied the therapeutic properties of the waters. It was Iasolino, however, who by testing balneothermal treatments and classifying the springs on the basis of the varying chemical composition of the waters launched real scientific studies of thermalism. Thus, in less than a century the springs became an important economic resource. The D'Avalos governors of Ischia themselves, gave impulse to this new activity, and in the seventeenth century a group of Neapolitan nobles established a hospice for the poor, Pio Monte della Misericordia, near the historic spring of Gurgitello and thermalism became a social service.

In the nineteenth century the springs at Casamicciola were already famous and attracted the European nobility in hordes. Even Giuseppe Garibaldi came for treatments in June 1864 and it is said that he was literally forgotten in the "Stufe di San Lorenzo" by his staff who were so fascinated by the landscapes.

Nor did the devastating earthquake of 1883 with its tragic wreath of destruction weaken the energies of the Ischians. The island's extremely mild climate, with a mean annual temperature of 17°C (that permits sunbathing even in the middle of winter) and the air that is rich in iodine and sodium chloride because of the sea, are the ideal complements to guarantee the complete success of the cures and treatments, with positive effects on the skin and nerve endings.

In the twentieth century the hotels and the villages where they are located quickly adjusted to the demands of health and beauty tourism, with beautiful, lush gardens, excellently equipped centers for disintoxication and beauty treatments that have focused the interest of countless international tour operators on Ischia. In this way, the island has managed to successfully exploit one of the world's richest and most interesting hydro-thermal assets. In fact, Ischia has twenty-nine hydro-thermal basins, over one hundred springs, and sixty-nine fumarole fields.

As the years went by, with advances in medicine and science (in this sense the Giulio Iasolino's discoveries seem distant indeed) the range of treatments and applications offered by Ischian facilities has gradually diversified and specialized leading to greater effectiveness. This diversification is dictated as much by organoleptic properties as by geographical location.

The most famous and effective basins include Casamicciola: the town is extremely rich in spas that have been renowned throughout the ages. The Romans who had placed the waters under the protection of the gods believed Apollo to be the tutelary deity of the Casamicciola springs. Legend has it that Ulysses landed at Casamicciola and regained his lost vigor in the waters of the Gurgitello.

There are three main thermo -mineral basins that feed many springs with different therapeutic properties. Gurgitello, for example, is located on the east side of Piazza Bagni, at the foot of the Ombrasco hill. The Romans were the first to call this smoking stream that flowed above ground into the sea near the pine grove of Pio Monte della Misericordia as it is known today, by the name *gurges*. The springs of the Ombrasco, with their interesting names, *Sorgente dell'Oro* [spring of gold], *del ferro* [iron], *dell'argento* [silver] and *del Cappone* all flow into it. The waters of the Gurgitello are clear, odorless, colorless and slightly alkaline; the temperature ranges from 65° to 80°C and are available at all the Piazza Bagni spas.

Other springs, including the Tamburo and Spelonca, flow

into the Cotto and Sinigallia (or Sinigaglia) basin on the west side of Piazza Bagni on the slopes of the Olivo and Pera hills. Here the temperature varies between 50° and 60°C, and the water is alkaline.

At the foot of the Cesa hill, on the west side of Casamicciola in a gorge known as Cava di La Rita is the La Rita basin: the salty tasting water ranges from 60° to 72°C.

Then there are waters for drinking cures that have been famous since the earliest times. In particular, there is the Enaniello water that springs in the Cognulo forests, Cappone water that comes from the Gurgitello and the Cava Fontana water that originates on the heights of Campomanno.

The hot springs of Castiglione draw from a local basin that extends over an area of more than 4000 square meters between the Bagnitiello hill and the beach at Cafiero. These saline-bromine-iodine waters reach a temperature of 70°C.

But, of course, there is more than Casamicciola. Even the town of Ischia boasts its own, important and famous spas: the Terme Comunali stands in Via Iasolino, practically opposite the Casina Reale. Until the mid-nineteenth century this was the site of the old baths, Formiello and Fontana. Actually, they were little more than two cabins, one for each spring and in spite of their low capacity were frequented by an ever increasing number of foreigners. The 1821 survey by the architect Benedetto Iovene, whom the city commissioned to prepare an estimate for restorations highlighted the total state of decay of the buildings. In 1823 the Municipal Council approved the plans by the architect De Fazio, but work only began in 1843 under the direction of a Mr. Fazzini. The spa was opened two years later. The main façade with its elegant

The famous Terme Poseidon at Citara di Forio.

smooth ashlar opens onto Via Iasolino, while the slightly protruding central portion, comprises three arches supported by column-flanked pilasters.

The area of Forio, also has some fine spa facilities: going along the street of the same name, we come to the Terme Castaldi where the radioactive chlorine-sulfate-sodium waters of the hot spring are used for baths, inhalations, irrigations and for preparing muds. The most important spa complex is the one at the Giardini Poseidon near the beach at Citara. Established thanks to the initiative of the Bavarian industrialist Ludwig Kuttner, with joint participation of the municipal government, these baths use the therapeutic properties of the waters that come from the island's volcanic viscera, with a complex of twenty pools situated on the garden's terraces at various altitudes.

As to Serrara Fontana, going down, we come to the beaches with the fumaroles, Cava Petrella, Cava Scura, the final part of Maronti and Sorgeto, with the natural hot pools and the modern spa that use the springs of Cava Scura, Nitrodi and Olmitello. The fumaroles on the Lido dei Maronti (a wide, 1700 meter long beach) are used for therapeutic purposes along with other minor phenomena of secondary volcanism. The most important springs are Nitrodi (or Nitruoli) and Olmitello. The former, that is located at 202 meters in the Buonopane district gets its name from the nymphs who were believed to have guarded the place and whose beauty could be attributed to the properties of the waters that are rich in nitron, that is soda. It was no coincidence that Giulio Iasolino attributed the beauties of the women of Barano to this spring. Nor is it a coincidence that the Roman temple dedicated to Eros, the god of love once stood

Grand Hotel Terme Regina Isabella, at Lacco Ameno.

here. The Olmitello spring, is situated at an altitude of 50 meters just next to the Lido di Maronti.

The waters from these two springs are radioactive, bicarbonate-sulfate and saline-iodine and suitable for various applications (baths, aerosol, whirlpools, muds) and are particularly indicated for rheumatic disorders as well as skin and respiratory diseases.

In fact, it is well worth emphasizing the extreme diversity that characterizes waters of Ischia. The offering includes grotto-therapy, inhalation therapy, and physiotherapy, as well as bath, shower and mud treatments, all of which upon request can be completed with specific treatments such as massages and therapeutic exercise to render the cures more effective and prolong their results.

Most of the muds here are of volcanic origin with a clayey component, that is they have a greater quantity of organic substances than clays from other sources. The solid substance is diluted with mineral water. The island's mineral waters are known for their high spring temperature, high radioactivity and high mineral content. These properties are particularly beneficial for treatments based on baths, that must be taken on an empty stomach, in pools or individual tubs, in waters that generally come to the surface at 40°C. The shower is an adjunct or alternative to the baths. These showers consist of thermal water, at pressures that can be adjusted to the specific needs, that massage the skin. There are also underwater showers where the spray is directed onto specific body parts with the patient already immerged in a thermal bath.

Grotto-therapy is a totally different thing. It is particularly widespread in Ischia where, in spite of its slightly "primitive" and unappealing name it is extremely relaxing. In essence it consists of a not too long (from a minimum of 10 to a maximum of 60 minutes) stay in natural caverns distinguished by a relatively high air temperature created by the nearby hot mineral springs. There are even differences between one grotto and another: there are particularly humid caverns, filled with steam from the springs and where the temperature does not usually exceed 40°C. They are natural Turkish baths and quite different from the "dry grotto" where, there is no moisture and the temperature can get as high as 70°C. These specific features are essential for establishing proper therapeutic use of the various caverns even though in general we can say that

grotto-therapy helps the metabolic functions by intensifying perspiration and triggering an increase in body temperature, it is beneficial to the cardiocirculatory and respiratory systems.

Inhalation therapy targets the respiratory tract. It aims at putting the airways in direct contact with high concentrations of mineral water that is atomized or fragmented into infinitely small particles with the aerosol technique, and into which atomized medicines can also be mixed. The nebulizations and inhalations can be induced artificially or they can be done by exploiting the appropriate natural settings.

A more "usual" treatment is physiotherapy, even though few people know that the ancient Romans helped the effects of the spring waters with mild exercise. Today, these applications are divided into massotherapy (done

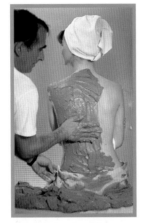

The Muds of Ischia

One of the most popular and effective treatments provided at Ischia's spas, is the application of volcanic mud that is softened and made pliable by the addition of the local mineral water. The mud packs that are from 10 to 12 cm thick, are applied to the body at a temperature of around 47°C. Each application must last for a good half hour. The mud is then carefully removed so that the patient can take a bath in mineral water. After the bath, there is a one hour rest period, during which the patient continues to perspire until the reaction is completed.

by hand or special machines with effects that are both localized and extended to the entire body), rub-downs (where the masseur's hands squeeze the tissues to help eliminate waste and improve oxygenation), as well as baths alternating hot and cold water which, in addition to the invigorating effects of the temperature changes, facilitate exercise since the body weighs less in water and there is thus less resistance. Combining the physical benefits of physiotherapy with the curative properties of the thermal applications, we obtain a complete cycle that is extremely salutary for the entire body. After two or three weeks of taking the cures, the effects are guaranteed and evident: the body is invigorated, agile and healthy, as is the spirit after a vacation in a charming, delightful place, in contact with absolutely uncontaminated nature and seas. What could be better than a sojourn on Ischia?

ISCHIA

I n addition to the main port and the town that has the same name as the island, **Ischia**, has long been identified with the fate of this little piece of volcanic ground that rises in the Tyrrhenian Sea. It has always been a privileged landing, and it is here that castle, complete with bastions, was built and was the theater of significant events and home of the island's rulers. Today, Ischia extends over 3 km in length between **Ischia Porto**, the coastal volcanic crater that has been transformed into a well-equipped harbor, and **Ischia Ponte** that owes its name to the bridge the Aragonese built to connect the village to the Isolotto del Castello.

THE CASTLE

The **Castle**, frequently called *Castrum Ieronis* or Castel Gerone, for the tyrant from Siracusa who probably built the first fortress on the island, has a rich history, and an interesting present, fine architecture and artistic worth. For centuries it was the strategic bulwark defending the Gulf of Naples.

We reach the structure that was sold to the state in 1912, and is now in private hands, via a 227 meter long causeway that was built between 1423 and 1438 by Alfonso of Aragon to replace the earlier and fragile wooden bridge. The *Batteria del Molo*, or battery of the wharf was situated at the end of the bridge, and on the terrace we can still see traces of the trapezoidal supports for the heavy artillery. On the right a large archway leads into the Castle.

The mighty Aragonese Castle towers over the Isolotto.

On the following pages: picturesque views of the Castle perched on the top of the cliff.

In order to reach the buildings on the rocks more safely, Alfonso of Aragon built a tunnel into the rock. The gallery that is 10 meters wide and 18 meters high runs for 427 meters; it has a series of lozenge-shaped openings. Even the fortified walls around the castle were built by king Alfonso in 1425 within the context of the major works that were needed to restore and transform the existing bulwark.

Midway along, we come to the **Chapel of San Giovangiuseppe della Croce**, the saint from Ischia who lived between the seventeenth and eighteenth centuries and was canonized in 1839.

If we go further up, we can enjoy a marvelous view that extends as far as Procida and the islet of Vivara. On the final rock we come to the ruins of the Castle **keep**: 80 meters above the sea, the main section is trapezoidal.

The Castle can be reached from Ischia via a long causeway; the north wing of the Castle seems to rise steeply from the sea.

The southern side of the Aragonese stronghold stretches out before us, with its fortifications and mighty crenellated walls protected by four cylindrical towers.

On the north it appears isolated and projects over the water. The southern part develops along a wide cliff enclosed by four crenellated cylindrical towers that are connected by walls. Constructed over a V century building the keep was entirely rebuilt by the D'Avalos family that became lords of the castle and of the entire island at the end of the XV century.

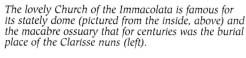

The lovely Church of the Immacolata is famous for its stately dome (pictured from the inside, above) and the macabre ossuary that for centuries was the burial place of the Clarisse nuns (left).

CHURCH OF THE IMMACOLATA

The **Church of the Immacolata**, that was once annexed to the Convent of the Clarisse nuns, was built in 1737. The abbess, Mother Battista Lanfreschi, wanted a new church to replace the small chapel dedicated to St. Francis. After the monasteries and religious orders were suppressed in 1803, this church, as well as the convent were abandoned.

The Greek-cross plan is augmented by a rectangular room on the main axis that is used as the presbytery, and another that serves as the pronaos. The beautiful dome, that is supported by four fluted columns with pairs of pilaster strips on the high drum, with curved tympanun windows, is easily recognizable even from afar.

The **Convent** is a rectangular block with a prospect embellished by orderly rows of windows. The wide terrace offers a beautiful panorama. An underground chamber is the *ossuary of the nuns*. Here, not even so long ago, it was possible to see rows of mummies that were still on impressive seats where the bodies of the dead were placed.

The Cathedral

The fourteenth century **Cathedral dell'Assunta** with its severe and forbidding contours still has its original nucleus in the underground *crypt*. The plan is rectangular with simple cross-vaults. There are interesting traces of *frescoes* probably done by artists close to the Giottesque masters who worked in Naples when the monumental building was under construction. Remains of decorative stucco work can be seen in the apse, where there is also the stone altar, and where the squared stone pillars that encompass the ancient lava stone (piperno) columns are also visible. The church was built at the end

The impressive ruins of what was the Cathedral of Ischia, and even today conserves traces of its former splendor.

of the XVII century and was beautified during the years of Monsignor Costigliola's episcopate. The building was entirely destroyed, along with the other buildings on the islet between 24 June and 21 August 1809, during the battle in which Murat defeated the English, and the devastating actions that followed it. On 27 June 1810 the services usually held in the cathedral were moved to the Church of Santa Maria della Scala that crowns the village of Ischia Ponte, just opposite the Castle.

The old cathedral still has traces of the stucco work that once comprised part of the decorations, and remains of interesting frescoes in the crypt.

Opposite page: picturesque view of the Isolotto that is rich in greenery, luxuriant gardens and romantic alleyways. Lower right: a view of the old Tempietto di San Pietro.

OTHER ARCHITECTURAL BEAUTIES OF THE ISOLOTTO

This small, but magnificent islet is dotted by other architectural jewels, such as the **Tempietto di San Pietro**. This compact building of squared blocks of piperno is a perfect hexagon. Hidden behind a high drum an extrados cupola crowns the building that was put up in 1547 under orders from Dionisio Basso, a wealthy gentleman who contributed a king's ransom, as it were, for this cause. Actually, what he did want was to acquire a benefice from the Roman Curia so that his son, a priest, could have a church of his own. In 1823, Ferdinando I added the Isolotto to his domains and the building was thus taken away from the Church.

Higher up with respect to San Pietro is the area of the **former prison** that is reached by going through a gate in the town wall. A low pronaos leads into the first room with barrel vaults that is divided in two by a wide arch where we can see the holes left by the massive gates that once stood here, and then to the next room, with barrel-vaults and narrow, barred windows. The two rooms were built in the XV century, but we do not know what they were originally used for: it became a district prison as a result of the royal decree with which it was decided to give the entire complex to the state. During the Risorgimento, that is Italy's struggle for independence and unification, the prison was temporary home to several famous patriots, including Poerio, Nusco, Spaventa and Settembrini.

Ischia Ponte, with its austere looking urbanistic arrangement extends towards the causeway that links the Isolotto and Castle to the mainland.

ISCHIA PONTE

The area known as **Ischia Ponte**, although densely urbanized, reveals stratifications of ancient origin that are still clearly legible in spite of the fact that at the end of the nineteenth century major works were done to improve sanitation and urbanization. In 1878 an entire row of fishermen's houses was demolished, and then others were built on the area of what is now Via San Giovangiuseppe della Croce. Other, albeit less significant, works included road building aimed at modifying the steep slopes to facilitate transportation and give the streets of the area drainage facilities and sidewalks. Through these projects the ancient village became part of the modern town.

Even though the Castle is considered the focal point of Ischia Ponte, the agglomerate before it is rich in unusual architecture. For example there is the **Torre dell'Orologio**, (or clock tower) the Town Hall, that separates two parallel streets. Behind the castle, in line with the rocks, the façades of the houses and of the cathedral seem to offer themselves to the sea as prospects on a main street: they comprise a wall, built so that it could be seen by the sailors who were approaching the harbor, and to afford a view of the sea from the houses.

The dome and original campanile of Santa Maria della Scala, tower above the houses of Ischia Ponte.

Santa Maria Della Scala

Today the cathedral of Ischia is **Santa Maria della Scala**. Its name is that of a much older church that was built between the XI and XII centuries and annexed to the Augustinian Monastery. Structural modifications were made as early as the XIV and XV centuries when the village population gradually began to rise again after the devastation caused by the earthquake that struck in 1301. Then, between 1600 and 1614 the church was rebuilt on a new plan with two entrances, one of which faced the castle. Not even this structure lasted very long however, since it was soon demolished, probably in order to reinforce the foundations.

A new church was erected around the middle of the eighteenth century. The work was assigned to Antonio Massinetti who completed it in 1751. Following the suppression of the religious orders in 1808 the Augustinians were removed and the church, with the authorization of the king, was raised to the status of cathedral on 17 July 1810. Today, the basilica has a lovely façade with two superimposed orders, ending in a fronton that seems to embrace them. The church is built in the shape of a Latin cross, with a large transept that is highlighted by the majestic dome with lantern. We must also mention the **bell tower** which, seen from the sea still vaunts the original features of a tower created to defend the port from invading barbarians. Only in the early sixteenth century did it officially become a bell tower. Built in the XV century and better known as the "Torre del Mar" or tower of the sea, like the others, it is a square, and its pumice and lava stone masonry is covered with plaster. With its eastern wall set against the cathedral presbytery, the tower rises three stories, with lava stone girders with slits and arcatures along the top order.

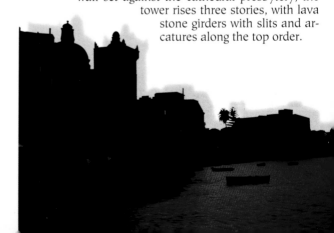

district's craftsmen. Another fine religious building is the **Church of the Annunziata**, that stands on Via Campagnano. The façade creates a lovely backdrop to the piazza located on the street that leads back up to Campagnano. And finally, there is the **Church of Sant'Antonio**, on the eponymous slope. Its current, single nave, structure dates from the eighteenth century, but the building was originally erected in 1225 at the same time as the Franciscan Monastery; it was destroyed by the eruption of 1301, then rebuilt and remodeled several times.

The majestic interior of the cathedral of Ischia Ponte that is renowned for its liturgical furnishings and some outstanding artworks such as a canvas by Giacinto Diano.

PALAZZO VESCOVILE

Along with the cathedral the archbishop's palace is the true center of religious power on Ischia. The building was erected in 1738 on the edges of the city, on land that belonged to the Gargiulo family, under the orders of Monsignor Schiaffinati who wanted to establish a seminary, which is precisely the purpose it served until 1865.

The palazzo, currently the seat of the bishopric, contains many marble fragments of great historic-artistic value, such as the early Christian bas-reliefs known as the *Sarcophagus of Ischia*, dating from the IV century AD and other marble slabs from the old *Cattedrale del Castello*, that can be seen in the atrium, the garden and other adjacent rooms.

THE CHURCHES OF ISCHIA PONTE

The Ponte area was densely populated even before the new Via Vittoria Colonna was built; it was here that the civil and economic life of the island flourished. The large number of churches in the district is yet further proof of how many people live and work here. On Via Mazzella there is the sixteenth century **Church of Spirito Santo**, that was formerly the chapel of the Cossa family. Going down a short but steep flight of steps we come to the **Confraternity of Santa Maria di Costantinopoli** (1629) that was established by the

The Mediterranean Houses

Along with its splendid noble palazzos, Ischia offers interesting examples of what is commonly known as "poor" or humble architecture. Closely packed houses crowed the shore facing the Castle, an old hamlet of merchants and fisherman that has survived to this day, embellished with corbels, arches, loggias and outdoor staircases. There are many of these "Mediterranean houses" along Via Giovanni da Procida. Here there are countless examples of this varied and spontaneous architecture that represents the ancient heart of Ischia.

ISCHIA PORTO

It is a fact that the **Ischia Porto** district, the heart of the island's business life and tourism was urbanized rather recently. Interest in the area only developed in the late eighteenth century and increased because Ferdinando II of the Two Sicilies was enthusiastic about the new and inviting harbor built in 1854, that cleverly exploited the natural loops of the old Lago dei Bagni. Actually, the lake touched the beaches of the Casina Reale (that was later converted into a spa and baths for the military), where the royal family would go on holiday. In 1792 queen Maria Carolina commissioned a tempera painting of the Lago dei Bagni, that portrayed the district's fishermen, for the study of king Ferdinando IV (who later became Ferdinando I of the Two Sicilies).

Among the many picturesque sites in the district, one street that runs parallel to the embarcaderos leads to the **Punta del Faro**, that offers a view reaching as far as Procida and Phlegraean Fields, then it continues to the **Church of Sant'Alessandro**, the **Spiaggia degli Inglesi** and the **Parco Termale di Castiglione** that is equipped with hot and cold pools that slope down to the sea. Near the Castiglione beach, inside a rather small grotto, you can take a dip in water that is heated by boric acid fumaroles in the lower rocks.

Ischia Porto is nestled in a well-protected natural cove, a longtime popular and privileged harbor.

The Feast of St. Alexander

One of the most popular events in the Is-chia Ponte district is, without a doubt, the feast of St. Alexander who was martyred during the reign of Maximinius. The saint's Passion is commemorated on 26 August, with a picturesque procession in historical costume that winds its way through the steep and narrow alleyways, fascinating visitors and the local population alike.

The other buildings we can admire from here include the **Church of Santa Maria di Portosalvo**. This too, was built by order of the sovereign Ferdinando II who promoted the urbanization of the area. The new settlement developed in full harmony with the older, historical Ponte district, where as late as the nineteen fifties transport ships were still allowed to dock.

Left, the beach at Ischia Porto is crowded on hot summer days. Right, from above: a view of the fishermen's port and beach. Below, a panorama that reaches from Punta del Faro to Procida and Phlegraean Fields.

A stroll through Ischia's lively streets and alleyways is a pleasant experience. Here you can find shops selling all kinds of merchandise, from antiques to locally grown fresh fruits and vegetables arranged in tempting displays. And here you can discover the true, friendly, cordial and generous spirit of the island's people.

Via Vittoria Colonna

The main street of the island's largest district, the fulcrum of the area, is named for a Roman noblewoman who became the glory of this little scrap of land that is embraced by the Tyrrhenian Sea. Vittoria Colonna, barely nineteen years old, was married to Ferdinando (or Ferrante) Francesco D'Avalos, marchese of Pescara and ruler of Ischia on 27 December 1509. The lavish wedding celebrations were held on the island, and most probably in the old cathedral that stood next to the castle, even though some sources maintain that some other, smaller churches were more likely settings. What is certain, however, is that this noblewoman who went down in history for the elegant verses she wrote, for the fact that she was loved by many of the era's most outstanding figures (with Michelangelo not the least of them), and for her deep religious faith, turned the Ischia Castle into a literary salon that was famed throughout Europe. She left a deep and indelible mark on the island's history.

The outside and interior of a small chapel where, according to one local tradition, Vittoria Colonna was married to Ferdinando Francesco D'Avalos.

Starting from the village of Ischia Porto, and following the road that runs parallel to the embarcadero, we can find some extraordinarily beautiful spots, such as the very green Sant'Alessandro district (above), the famous Spiaggia degli Inglesi (left) and another favorite of sun worshippers and bathers, the beach known as Spiaggia di San Pietro (below).

Opposite page: different views of the church of San Pietro, at Ischia Porto with its unusual curved façade, and the tympanum that follows the elliptical lines of the building.

THE CHURCH OF SAN PIETRO

Set back with respect to the port on what is not quite a square, at the top of a short flight of stops, the **Church of San Pietro**, also known as "Del Purgatorio" is a unique sight with is convex façade, and the tympanum that follows the curve of the elliptical plan. It was built in 1781, perhaps it was commissioned by the parish priest, Antonio Morandi, at a time when there were no churches in the Ischia Porto district. Items of interest inside are the semicircular chapels, while the presbytery opens in a rational, rectangular space, with a barrel vault that is lower than the rest of the church. The architecture is definitely original and anything but static or provincial – a true "modern" jewel of its era.

THE CHURCH OF SAN GIROLAMO

Not far from the church of San Pietro we come to the **Church of San Girolamo**. Built of tufa and lava stone, with a painted stucco exterior, it was donated to the priests of Santa Maria della Scala by the Municipality of Ischia on 7 March 1543. It is a simple structure with a single nave and a barrel vault; the façade was remodeled in the neoclassical style at the end of the nineteenth century.

THE CHAPEL OF SAN PIETRO

On the hillside east of the port we find the **Chapel of San Pietro**, the only surviving evidence of an early Basilian monastery built some time

around the year 1000. It was abandoned after the volcanic eruption of 1301 and suppressed in the XVI century so that another could be built. The benefits and title of abbey were transferred to the little hexagonal church known as *Tempietto di San Pietro*. In spite of this, the chapel on the hill of San Pietro was restored just a few years later, but by 1740 it had been demolished. The simple structure we see today was commissioned by the owner of the land and built over the original site in 1860.

29

The Local Festivals

Ischia's patron saint is Giovangiuseppe della Croce and his feast is the first Sunday in September. It is celebrated with a series of events that last for three or four days: for the occasion there is picturesque lighting out

along the streets and a long procession of boats accompanies the statue of the saint from Ischia Porto to the Ponte district. Another popular event, that draws countless visitors, is the feast of St. Anne, 26 July. It is a "rite of the sea" that ends with the "burning of the Aragonese Castle", an allegorical pageant of boats and lavish fireworks.

Thick, lush pine groves are a typical feature of Ischia. The grove known as "Pineta di Porto di Ischia" that developed through the centuries over an ancient lava flow is particularly beautiful.

THE PINE GROVES

Ischia's fertile hillsides, along with huge blocks of lava stone that are living proof of the volcanic eruptions that for centuries ravaged the island, are often covered with thick **pine groves**. Most of the trees are umbrella and cluster pines and they were planted thanks to the foresightedness of the Bourbon rulers. One of the most beautiful is the grove that overlooks Ischia Porto and Ischia Ponte. It is the "child" of a famous father, the Neapolitan botanist, Giovanni Gussone, who earned the well-deserved admiration and respect of the Bourbon court in Naples because of his work developing the grove in the XIX century. His brilliance is still evident today in the flourishing canopies of these trees whose shade has led to the development of rich forest undergrowth.

THE ANCIENT AQUEDUCT

One of the typical problems of island life in general is a constant supply of fresh water. Ischia, however, with its wonderful – and not only thermal – water resources has never had to face this issue. Clear evidence of this can been seen in the monumental Spanish **aqueduct** that runs along the hills of Ischia Ponte, up the slopes towards Campagnano, to the rocks of Sant'Anna. The double order of majestic arches runs parallel to the road offering an unusual backdrop to the city. Water for the villages of Ischia and Casamicciola comes from the rich springs of Buceto, at the foot of a hill covered with lush chestnut groves, Colle Ietto, that rises to a height of 589 meters.

The majestic arches of Ischia's ancient aqueduct wind their way across the island.

Ischia and the Sea

Ischia has every right to be proud of its centuries-long relationship with the sea. Today, that sea means tourism, windsurfing, scuba diving and a bevy of centers for catamaran, canoeing, and sailing enthusiasts. In the past, however, the sea meant trade and commerce, tall ships docking and islanders dedicated to seafaring. Even today, although cargo and passenger traffic have taken on another dimension with respect to the past, traditions still survive, in the water taxis that ride the waves to satisfy a tourist or to meet the needs of one the island's residents.

Fishing

Even though the northern side of the island, with its many beaches and moorings, with low coasts that gently sweep below the surface of the sea stretching into a broad platform, has always had a privileged relationship with the sea, with waters particularly suitable for fishing, this activity has never been as significant for Ischia's economy as, let us say, farming. And now, the number of islanders in the fishing business is lower than ever. Ischia Ponte is the fishing boat center par excellence, and is "home" to over half the island's fishermen. It is followed, at a respectful distance, by Forio, Sant'Angelo, Testaccio and Lacco Ameno. The less favorable areas are on the eastern coasts that lack good harbors, and the southern coast where the water is already very deep just a short distance from the shore. May to October is best season for fishing, but there are more than a few local fishermen who, in mid-summer,

leave their home waters for the better fishing grounds of the middle and upper parts of the Tyrrhenian.

32

Farming on Ischia

Even though it is an island, Ischia's economy has always been linked to its abundant and diversified agriculture. In fact, a large part of maritime traffic, the tall ships that sailed for Civitavecchia and Genoa for centuries carried Ischia's fine produce: outstanding fruits and vegetables. The entire Forio district has long been a major farming center. As the years went by and the spas developed, with the gradual growth of the tourist industry that could guarantee higher income with less effort than fishing or farming, agriculture has slowly been abandoned. The only sector that seems able to withstand this trend is the one that for centuries was the island's main crop: grapes. Vines may have been imported by the ancient Greek settlers, or perhaps even earlier. Ischia's wines have always been renowned and comprised one of the leading products among the islands export, and hence a significant economic resource. In recent times, when interest in agriculture in general was diminishing, the repeated crises that struck the grape and wine market – and prices – pointed Ischia towards other crops. Aside from the large vineyards that flourished on the hillsides, the others were replaced with more profitable crops that were easier and faster to sell. In spite of all this, agriculture is still vital to a larger part of Ischia's population, especially the people who live on the southern part of the island – that is the part with the more difficult ground that has been harder for the progress that has come with the development of the tourist industry to penetrate. These are the people who continue to conserve and hand down the centuries old farming tradition of the island: every year they harvest incomparable, fine and wholesome produce.

Island Traditions

Like many places with ancient origins, this island, too is linked to old traditions. They are traditions tied to the sea, to historical events that have been transformed into legend and local festivals: such as the feasts of Saint John the Baptist and Saint Anne, and the ancient propitiatory rituals that have become part of the island's folklore. One of the most famous of these is the dance of the "N'drezzata". Its secrets comprise a true heritage that is passed down from generation to generation among the residents of Buonopane who dedicate lengthy preparations to its performance. This tradition appears so deeply rooted that a "piccola N'drezzata", performed by children ranging from six to ten years of age has recently been created.

CASAMICCIOLA

For those who arrive by sea, **Casamicciola**, one of the towns on the northern side of Ischia appears like a long green curve, dominated by Epomeo and enclosed between Punta La Scrofa and the Gran Sentinella hill that overlooks the harbor. The municipality is divided into six sections: *Marina* and *Perrone* on the sea (Casamicciola bassa), *Bagni, Maio, Sentinella* and *La Rita* on the hill (Casamicciola alta). The **pleasure port** that comprises a double wharf opens onto Piazza Parina, the main square and the center of the town's business and social life where the main stores, cafes and trattorias are located.

The place name is said to derive from the joining of the word "casa" and the name "Miccio" of Medieval origin. In any event, tradition speaks in favor of another, more interesting etymology, linked to the name of a poor cripple, Nisula or Nizzola who was miraculously cured by the thermal waters.

Ancient Greek chronicles date the earliest human settlements of Casamicciola in the Iron and Bronze ages. The Greek colonists, who came from Chalcis and Eretria in several waves between the XI and VIII centuries BC, probably settled near Marina and introduced the art of pottery making that fueled flourishing trade with other Mediterranean coastal peoples.

After a long period of bradyseismic and telluric phenomena, it was the Cumaeans who settled in what is now the Perrone district. Between the II and III centuries AD the Romans settled at Fundera and on the Gran Sentinella hill, as we can see from interesting archeological finds that include the ruins of a villa.

It is not, however, possible to reconstruct Casamicciola's role in Ischia's history during the High Middle Ages up to the XIII century with any certainty at all. We do know that a series of earthquakes caused great upheavals on the island between 1225 and 1275. The village only began to prosper again in the sixteenth century thanks to Giulio Iasolino who rediscovered the curative powers of the **waters** of Casamicciola. Actually, it was as in the fourteenth century that Giovanni da Casamicciola, personal physician to Charles of Anjou studied, albeit, superficially, the therapeutic potential of those waters. However, it was only Iasolino who undertook the first studies of thermalism that could be considered scientific. Thus, in a short time, the springs became an important economic resource and enjoyed the favor of the D'Avalos governors of the island. In fact, in the seventeenth century, as we have mentioned, a group of Neapolitan nobles founded a hospice for the poor known as **Pio Monte della Misericordia** near the **Gurgitello spring**, giving this activity an innovative social value.

Today Casamicciola is a charming spot steeped in greenery; it owes its appearance to the massive reconstruction work done following the terrible earthquake of 1883. The town stretches gracefully behind the port.

Fishing, the harbor and tourism are the key resources of Casamicciola's economy. Along with the famous Parco Termale del Castiglione (opposite page), Casamicciola still conserves places of incomparable charm and picturesque beauty.

The eighteenth century was a golden period for Casamicciola: villas and hotels were built near the **springs of Gurgitello**, **Cotto** and **La Rita**, flowering gardens embellished **Piazza Bagni**, **Piazza Maio**, **Marina** and **Perrone**. This propensity for tourism was further strengthened in the nineteenth century when the village became one of the most famous spa resorts in Italy.

The town's rise, however, came to an abrupt halt when the earthquake of 28 July 1883 devastated the entire island. Casamicciola lost its famous visitor facilities and the villas built for the elite tourists. The often indiscriminate demolition work, dictated by fears of a new cataclysms eliminated the surviving historical and environmental treasures. The reconstruction was a turning point: only a few areas were restored according to conservative criteria. Many others were expanded in a grandiose and innovative manner that gave the town its delightful and welcoming atmosphere that distinguish it even today. Even the churches that arouse the visitor's interest are the result of this radical reconstruction. The **Parish Church of Santa Maria Maddalena** we see today replaced the old church, also dedicated to the Magdalene, that was completely destroyed by the earthquake of 1883. The original church was located a little farther uphill and was an extension of the small, fourteenth century church of San Severino that had been remodeled in 1540.

The **Church of the Immacolata**, of modest size with a single nave, was built at the beginning of the twentieth century to replace an eighteenth century house of worship, dedicated to Saint Anthony that collapsed during the earthquake. On the Marina we see the **Church of the Madonna del Buon Consiglio** that the sailors wanted built. It is decorated with stucco work, and has three polychrome marble altars and pilasters faced with marble from Mondragone. The church is also named for St. John the Baptist in whose honor the sailors used to celebrate a noisy festival on 24 June.

Among Casamicciola's attractions we cannot forget **Castiglione** strategically situated between the hills and the sea. The area has been extensively studied because of the volcanic features of the ground and the presence of ancient human settlements. The place name probably refers to a fortified citadel built by the Cumaean colonists. According to one legend, the Cumaean Sibyl, bathed in these waters and foretold the birth of the Messiah. Among the rocks were can still see a small cavern known as the *Sibyl's Cave*, to recall this tradition. Castiglione is rich in mineral water springs that have long been used and frequented. It has conserved its reputation through the centuries, partly because of many illustrious visitors that include Pliny, Julius Cesar, Robert of Anjou, Boccaccio and Ferdinando IV of Bourbon. After a period of marked decline, Castiglione's reputation flourished again: Lamartine, Garibaldi and Ibsen were among those who took a dip among the rocks, and since then the place has remained famous. Today, the entire area comprises the famous and highly popular **Parco Termale del Castiglione**.

The Earthquake of 1883

The terrible earthquake of 1883 literally devastated life in all the villages on Ischia. In addition to killing 1,784 people and injuring about 500, it ravaged the village buildings and destroyed documents that had been conserved for over a thousand years. It generated a wave of feelings and solidarity that quickly swept over Italy. In this dramatic situation, it was the press that spread the news – and sensations – with front page stories dedicated to the tragedy. The event resounded throughout the country with such strength that soon the name "Casamicciola" became a synonym for "total ruin."

LACCO AMENO

Lacco Ameno is shaped like an amphitheater embracing a small anchorage on the northern coast of Ischia. This beach and spa resort stretches between the tip of Monte Vico, the slopes of Epomeo and the Fundera plateau. It is to this shape that it owes its name, "Lacco" which derives from the Greek *laccos* meaning "cavity." The designation Ameno was only added in 1863.

In addition to being the island's smallest township, Lacco Ameno is the site of *Pithecusa*, the oldest settlement on Ischia founded in the VIII century BC. The site has been pinpointed as having been on the top and eastern slopes of Monte Vico, the former acropolis, at the extreme edge of the current town. The two coves of San Montano and Sotto Varule were the trading and military ports, respectively, while the San Montano valley was the necropolis.

Pithecusa, the first Greek colony in southern Italy and the farthest western point of Greek expansion must have been very important as we can see from the huge amount of archeological finds: ruins of Hellenic walls, the foundation stones of a temple, parts of private dwellings. In particular on the Piana di Santa Restituta, there are remains of brick yards; pottery and metals give evidence of the settlement's diversified, and probably prosperous trading and manufacturing activities. The different provenances of the finds, from various cultures (Greek, Egyptian, Syrian and Etruscan) also confirm *Pithecusa's* role as a trading center that served to vehicle many elements of Greek culture, from the alphabet, to the potter's wheel, to grape and olive growing that were absorbed by the peoples of Campania.

The establishment of Cumae, on the Campania coast halted the development of the settlement which, did however, continue to play a leading role thanks to its flourishing crafts that were famous for terracotta and metal wares as well as jewels

Pithecusa began its decline around the II century BC due to several causes that included the violent eruptions of Epomeo and the development of the Greek colony *Neapolis*. Although it had been identified during the last years of the eighteenth century, it remained practically unexplored until the middle of the twentieth if we do not count the nineteenth century excavations of some tombs. In fact, the first attempts at excavations at San Montano brought to light a vast **necropolis**. The area extends over 1200 square meters and contains more than 1300 tombs that can be dated from the VIII century BC to the II century AD. The objects buried with the dead provide important information as to the colony's social structure: it consisted primarily of craftsmen, merchants, middlemen and farmers. During the Roman era a residential settlement known as *Heraclion*, perhaps from the ancient cult dedicated to Hercules, developed over the site of the former *Pithecusa*. There must have been many villas overlooking the sea on the slopes of Monte Vico. The ruins of three rooms of one

The harbor and coast at Lacco Ameno where even a sunset is a breathtaking sight.

of these villas has survived and we can admire the geometric patterns on the mosaic floors.

There are traces of a lively settlement dating from the early centuries of the Christian era as well. Life around the new basilica must have been busy, and it remained so until at least the IX century when a gradual decline, probably triggered by telluric events as well as pirate raids, struck not only the official structures, but also the village of Lacco that was too exposed to the attackers. This may have been the reason that its inhabitants moved to the nearby hills of Mezzavia, Cementara, Casa Monte and Monte Vico. The fabric of the island's settlements was profoundly torn and life became a matter of expediency and day-to-day survival. The Medieval village grew up around the **Church of Santa Restituta** and the **Oratory of Count Marino**.

Up through the sixteenth century, Lacco and the adjacent villages remained in second place with respect to Ischia. Notwithstanding its limited size, in many eighteenth century documents the village was identified as "Lacco di Sopra" [upper Lacco] and "Lacco di vascio" [lower Lacco], a distinction that still exists between the hillside and seaside areas. During that period Lacco's economy enjoyed a revival. Grape growing expanded, and tomato farming developed: the tomato had been imported from the Americas.

Another resource, obviously, was fishing. The first tuna processing plant on Ischia dates from this period; it was located near the extreme tip of Monte Vico. In addition, starting in the seventeenth century, the fame of the **thermal springs** began to spread, bringing common folk and famous individuals to Lacco. The distinguished visitors included the Bavarian royal family , the duke of Atri and the duke of Acquaviva. The earthquake of 1883 that razed Casamicciola to the ground spared the coastal portion of Lacco, but severely damaged the inland districts of Rosario, Fundera, Fango, Pannella, Casa Pera and Mezzavia triggering major processes of transformation on this side of the island. It marked the beginnings of dynamic expansion favored by the morphology of the land, the natural harbors and increased tourist flow to the thermal springs. The greatest impulse came on the northern side thanks partly to the construction of roads such as the Casamicciola-Lacco coastal road, built in 1926. This led to the concentration of homes along the coast that was less damaged by the quake and easier to reach. Private construction in Lacco developed along what is now Via Roma and Piazza Santa Restituta that became the fulcrum of town life which previously had centered around the inland roads, Ebdonnade and Rosario, thus the definitive shift from fishing harbor to urban town was completed.

The Church of Santa Maria delle Grazie

On the Lacco marina in a picturesque environmental setting, but rather squashed by the agglomerate of surrounding homes stands the **Church of Santa Maria delle Grazie**. Documentary evidence of this church dates from the end of the seventeenth century. Built by the Monti family and donated to the curia in 1886 it was remodeled and enlarged several times during the course of the centuries so that only the arched lava portals of the original structure remain.

The church is built in the shape of a Latin cross with a single vaulted nave and a wide apse. The smaller dome that rises above the choir behind the main altar is decorated with stucco work; the larger one, over the transept rests on finely shaped pillars. There are six chapels under the lateral arches. Along with the rest of the building the *façade* with its clearly baroque lower order was severely damaged by the earthquake of 1883. After it was restored, the church was unexpectedly closed to the public and transformed into a warehouse. Only after World War II was Santa Maria delle Grazie returned to its original function as a house of worship and in 1949 was made the parish church to replace the existing Santissima Annunziata alla Fundera. During the following decades the church was subjected to extensive work, mainly on the bell tower, the organ and the marble basilican altar.

The Aragonese Tower

The peak of Monte Vico, the village's true scenic backdrop can be reached via a steep road that affords a view of the entire northern coast of the island. Monte Vico, that reaches a modest height of 116 meters is dominated by the fifteenth century **Aragonese Tower**. Built as a lookout and defensive structure in an era when Turks and pirates were a constant menace, and set on a solid base of 60 square meters, it was in a state of total abandon for such a long time that even the Aragonese crenellations were removed and used to build the walls of the nearby cemetery. Following the restorations that were begun in 1971 the tower has recovered its original appearance and continues to dominate the enchanting Baia di San Montano.

Opposite page: top a panorama of Lacco Ameno against the backdrop of the lush greenery of Monte Vico. Bottom: the splendid Baia di San Montano seen from the top of Monte Vico.

The harbor at Lacco Ameno with tightly packed white houses.

Following pages: the unmistakable Mushroom, symbol of Lacco Ameno rises from the blue sea.

THE MUSHROOM

The bay opposite Lacco is dominated by a most unusual rock formation: the 10 meter high **mushroom**. It is said that it fell off Monte Epomeo, and it has long been the symbol of the town. In order to counteract the erosion caused by the wind, sea and rainfall, a project was launched in 1987 to consolidate this amazing rock.

The Complex of Santa Restituta

The **Santa Restituta Complex** that consists of the church and adjacent chapel overlooks the piazza of the same name. The church's single nave is embellished with pairs of wood-faced semi-columns with Ionic stucco work capitals. The coffered ceiling hides the trussed vault. A richly crafted marble balustrade delimits the apse which is topped by a dome. The apse chapel is a single, barrel-vaulted room divided by a huge arch decorated with geometric stucco work.

It is not rash to say that in its various stratifications (pagan temple, early Christian basilica, high Medieval oratory, late Medieval chapel) and subsequent structural transformations this monumental complex embodies thousands of years of Lacco's history.

During the final years of the fifteenth century there were actually two adjacent *chapels* that were restored and re-floored with terracotta and majolica tiles. The gilded *statue of Santa Restituta*, also known as "La torca" that stands in a niche on the main altar of the right side chapel, replacing the old image of the saint also dates

The interesting Complex of Santa Restituta that overlooks the piazza of the same name. The archeological museum, that was opened in the mid-twentieth century is part of the complex.

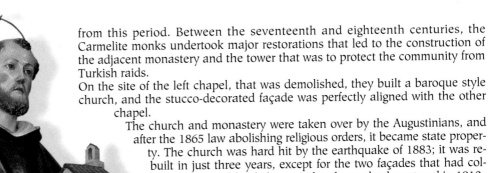

from this period. Between the seventeenth and eighteenth centuries, the Carmelite monks undertook major restorations that led to the construction of the adjacent monastery and the tower that was to protect the community from Turkish raids.

On the site of the left chapel, that was demolished, they built a baroque style church, and the stucco-decorated façade was perfectly aligned with the other chapel.

The church and monastery were taken over by the Augustinians, and after the 1865 law abolishing religious orders, it became state property. The church was hard hit by the earthquake of 1883; it was rebuilt in just three years, except for the two façades that had collapsed and could only be considered completely restored in 1910.

Near the church is the **Museo Archeologico di Santa Restituta**. The museum was established in the mid-twentieth century in concomitance with the beginning of the excavations that brought to light interesting structural elements dating from the Hellenistic, Roman and Early Christian eras. In the museum, in addition to items found on site, there are also finds from other places: Neolithic pieces and fossil shells found at 20 meters above sea level; Procidian fragments from the Bronze Age, pottery from Monte Vico and objects dating from the Roman era.

Some of the fine objects in the archeological museum (opposite page) including amphorae and an ancient Greek loom.

Tourism at Lacco Ameno

Starting in the 'fifties, tourism has become Lacco's main economic resource causing a shift that has profoundly modified the town's social, residential and economic life. The old fishing village originally targeted at an elite clientele, with grand hotels and prestigious homes, such as the eighteenth century Villa Arbusto and the adjacent Villa Gingerò, perched on the hill of the same name, or the princely homes on Monte Vico. Then, in the sixties, Lacco managed to acquire its reputation as the most chic spot on the island, a true refuge for the international jet-set. Only later was the town's economy to turn to mass tourism focused primarily on the beaches and countryside. Today, a stay in one of the typical places on the Corso, can be a pleasant diversion for the visitor, and the district's charming restaurants offer enticing

specialties. As to the sea, the Baia di San Montano, with its sandy beaches, warm waters, and splendid environmental setting, is one of the most beautiful places on the entire island. The health-giving springs of Santa Restituta, Regina Isabella, and the more recently discovered waters of Fundera and Fango continue to attract numerous visitors, mainly from abroad.

FORIO

The town of **Forio** rises on a promontory on the western coast of the island of Ischia, that extends inland as far as the middle-high slopes of Monte Epomeo.

The place name has been related to the Greek work *chorion*, village, even if the past scholars, considering the fertility of the land used the Greek *phoros*, and then the Latin *ferax* to describe the place.

Ever since ancient times, Forio has been one of the most important towns on the western part of the island, thanks to its wealth of thermal-mineral springs and its fertile soil.

According to some scholars, the first to settle the area were the Siracusans who built a temple dedicated to Venus Citarea whose memory survives in the current name of the Citara beach. They were followed by the Parthenopeans and then the Romans. During the times of Julius Caesar, the Sicilians, who claimed to have descended from the Siracusans, reestablished themselves here.

Its position, however, made the spot a great target for invaders, and over the centuries, this danger prompted the residents to build defensive towers and to extend their settlements inland towards higher ground.

As to the Medieval period, there is but little and then fragmentary information. However, the sources agree as to the identification of small inhabited centers scattered throughout the island.

The structure of the coastal village did provide the settlement with defenses against pirate raids. These forays were so frequent even in the XV century that in 1433 Alfonso of Aragon reinforced the castle fortifications and took measures to protect the more exposed parts of the island. Forio alone had nine towers.

The Aragonese period was also characterized by the granting of privileges that highlight the status of "free land" that had been guaranteed to Ischia. In this way, Alfonso and his successors tried to demonstrate their benevolence for the place; they enjoyed pleasant so-

A detail of the rocks that dominate the beach of San Francesco.

journs here and passed their time hunting and fishing. Among the various privileges, they granted property rights over a half mile of sea and all the beaches, and the promontory from which it was possible to earn considerable amounts to private citizens to set up tuna processing plants. For more than three centuries this concession was one of the main resources of the people, since permission to fish within a radius of "a half mile" included an obligation to sell one third of the catch at a fixed price that even the poor could afford.

Archive documents concerning the island during the period of the Viceroy, that is after 1559 testify to the clear dominance of the town of Ischia around the Castle, and Forio. The latter settlement was frequently damaged by marauding Turks, but reconstruction was intensive, and included an expansion of the town's defenses which, by 1558, included twelve towers.

The construction of the new **Convent of San Francesco** and the expansion of the **Complex of Santa Maria di Loreto** also date from this period. In a social context such as the one on this island, the religious architecture was a fundamental reference point. The areas in front of the houses of worship were systematically used a meeting places.

Between the seventeenth and eighteenth centuries the island's appearance changed, with many projects that had a decisive impact on the architecture and residential areas. This was especially true for Ischia Ponte and Forio which appeared to Berkeley in 1717 as "true cities" where stately homes, based on the "town-house model" stood and which by that century had attained a level of subdued elegance.

Between the XVIII and XIX centuries, like the rest of Ischia, Forio began to be mentioned in guidebooks, and in the *Grand Tour* literature. It became one of the favorite subjects of nineteenth century *vedute* and a constant destination – even through the twentieth century – for literati and painters. Under Bourbon rule the Island of Ischia seemed to be part of the Neapolitan cultural climate.

In 1743, Don Pietro Regine ordered the construction of **Cappella Regine**, a building dedicated to St. Philip Neri, in the greatest Neapolitan baroque tradition, with a slightly rococo air. Unfortunately, this building was demolished.

A stupendous overview of the coastline that runs from Lacco Ameno to Forio, a natural setting of incomparable beauty.

The village of Forio and its harbor nestled against the slopes of Monte Epomeo.

The suppression of the monastic orders during the decade of French domination led to the abandonment of religious buildings. Many were used for other purposes, such as the Franciscan Monastery in Forio that became the Town Hall.

During the nineteenth century as the island's towns continued to grow, and become more and more separate from the countryside, the need for a road that would link the

Above the famous "San Francesco" beach, one of the most popular in the area.
Right: behind Forio, the striking Punta Imperatore thrusts into the sea.

towns became a pressing issue. In 1881 the Forio Town Council proposed the creation of a consortium with the towns of Barano and Serrara-Fontana to share the expenses and to build two urban stretches of road: Piazza-San Sebastiano and San Gaetano-Piazza.

The earthquake of 1883 spared the part of Forio situated on the coast, but it destroyed the inland centers such as Monterone. The subsequent

The sea and fishing are vital to the entire of Ischia, and of course to Forio, where the waters are crowded with fishing boats.

reconstruction work affected other parts of the municipal territory which up to then were uninhabited.

In 1925 Forio became the capital of the district of the same name when the island was administratively divided into two districts: Ischia and Forio. Since that time the village has followed in the footsteps of the growth enjoyed by the island's bigger towns where the farm economy, based essentially on grape growing, has been supplemented by an increasingly important tourist component, especially in the years since 1950. Even for Forio, the growth of the spas and popularity of the hot springs played a vital role as they draw huge numbers of Italian and foreign visitors.

Notwithstanding work done after the earthquake of 1883, Forio maintained its physiognomy more or less intact until at least the nineteen sixties thanks to the strong blend of the Medieval and the "modernization" work of the XVII and XVIII centuries. The building boom of the following decades brought about some major changes, and the enormous amount of concrete that was poured did, in fact, compromise the traditional equilibrium that existed between the historic center and the countryside.

However, in spite of all this, Forio's urban layout and environmental setting are undisputedly lovely, whether we are looking at the historic center, the beaches or the inland areas.

THE CHURCH OF SAN GAETANO

The **Church of San Gaetano**, built in 1655 stands in Piazza Luca Balsofiore. It was the concrete fruit of the deep religious feelings of Forio's sailors and fishermen. They have remained deeply attached to this church as we can see from the many *ex voto*, in the form of model XVI-II century sailing ships and boats that adorn the pendentives of the dome. The main *façade* is definitely unusual as it narrows towards the top in relation to the counterforts on the sides. A triangular tympanum surmounts the grey lava stone portal. Above the tympanum, in the middle there is a window with rounded corners. Large scrolls join the aedicula to the end cornice. The raised arch dome that is divided into sections by wide ribs rises on a cylindrical drum around which there are four windows. The *interior* is shaped like a Latin cross with a large transept. On the sides of the single nave, three arches are supported by a row of pilaster strips against the columns. The upper section of the polygonal apse is decorated with high relief stucco *Angels and Clouds*. A double, unsymmetrical staircase leads to the church entrance.

The Church of San Gaetano with its unusual façade that narrows towards the top and its segmented dome, overlook Piazza Balsofiore.

60

The center of Forio, with its narrow streets and typical architecture of solemn, imposing palazzos. Throughout the year, the streets are lively and crowded with countless visitors and as well as the local population.

Corsa dell'Angelo

One of the island's dearest traditions is the "Race of the Angel" that is held the streets of Forio, Casamicciola and Lacco Ameno on Easter Monday. It is a religious pageant focused on the statue of the Angel who announces the Resurrection, and the statues of Christ and the Virgin Mary.

THE TOWER

The **Tower** can definitely be considered one of the most interesting civil buildings in Forio. It is the most important of the many towers that dot the town's territory. Built in 1480, just a few years after Barbarossa's terrifying raids, in the XIX century the Tower used as a prison. Later it was converted into a museum that houses sculptures and paintings by the local artist, Giovanni Maltese.

This circular structure has three stories and is part of a tight network of interesting buildings that include the **Palazzetto di vico Torrione** an eighteenth century structure that was remodeled in 1865.

THE ARCHICONFRATERNITY OF SANTA MARIA VISITAPOVERI

Next to the church of San Francesco, in the right corner of the Piazza del Municipo stands the **Arciconfraternita di Santa Maria Visitapoveri** that is deemed to have been founded in 1614. The furnishings and decorations were destroyed in the fire of 1670. The delicate *stucco decorations* were done when the building was being repaired after the fire.

The oratory has two *façades*: an outer one with a peperino stone portal decorated with aligned arches, a split fronton with an oval in the middle that is surmounted by a base that supports a wrought iron cross. The inner façade, that faces the atrium has an aedicula flanked by two pinnacles. The interior of the Arciconfraternita has a single nave that is rather low, with wooden stalls all around. The lunettes in the barrel-vault frame six oval paintings that are further enhanced by decorative stucco work. A bowl-shaped dome above the altar crowns the building. The oratory attained its greatest splendor in the XVIII century. The

The mighty, circular Tower of Forio.

painter, Alfonso di Spinga, was a member of the confraternity from 1747 and held various offices; between 1756 and 1774 he executed the oval paintings that depict the *Mysteries of the Virgin Mary* that are in the groins of the barrel-vault. The cantoria and the majolica floor were completed in 1791 which is when the organ was also installed.

The double façade and the elegant nave with wooden stalls and barrel-vault, of the Arciconfraternita di Santa Maria Visitapoveri.

The Church of Santa Maria del
Soccorso, perched on high above the
sea, is reached by a double staircase
that is with majolica tiles.

THE CHURCH OF SANTA MARIA DEL SOCCORSO

The **Church of Santa Maria del Soccorso** is located in the western section of the Forio town center, on a broad terrace overlooking the sea. The parvis, has a double, semicircular piperino stone staircase, with railings decorated with antique majolica tiles.

The *façade* follows the curved lines of the barrel-vault and is surmounted by the base that supports the central cross. The portal, with its piperino stone architraves creates a break in the gleaming whiteness of the façade. The *interior* is rather bare, since the only decorative elements are rustic Corinthian pilaster strips and simple frames that hold the *ex voto* that are models of sailing ships.

Details of the exterior of the Church of Santa Maria del Soccorso, from the votive crosses to the splendid majolica tiles, to the simple yet elegant architecture of the façade.

The simple interior of Santa Maria del Soccorso, contains many ex voto in form of sailing ships, and a large wooden crucifix. Right: an interesting picture of the altar decorated with wheat to celebrate Easter.

On the left side we can see the large *Chapel of the Crucifixion* with is cross-vault. The chapel is enclosed by a marble balustrade with a wrought iron railing. The wooden *crucifix* was found in the sea after a storm in the early XVI century. On the ceiling, fifteen *angels-putti* with hammers, nails, pliers and a crown of thorns symbolize the martyrdom of Jesus.

Originally, this church was part of an Augustinian monastery that was founded in 1350 and suppressed in 1653. At that time, it comprised only the central nave, there was no chapel in the apse, nor was there a dome above the altar, these additions were built in 1791 and 1854, respectively. A new, smaller dome was built after the earthquake of 1883.

Sometimes, when the sun sets into the sea, if you stand on the terrace you can see the "green beam". There are many conflicting explanations for this famous optical phenomenon, but it is generally agreed that it is a good omen.

THE BEACH OF CITARA

Along with the chestnut and pine groves, Forio boasts yet another attraction: the lush **Giardino Esotico Gancia**. And then, the long and famous **beach of Citara** with its fine white sands, stretching beyond the promontory of Santa Maria del Soccorso as far as the spur of Punta Imperatore, deserves special mention. The beach appears dotted with rocks emerging from the sea; it stretches along a beautiful bay that is protected by the hills of Capizzo and Cuotto. In ancient times it was dedicated to Venus Citarea (who was worshipped here along with Apollo the Healer), and today the beach is famous for its natural beauty, and its thermal waters (46°-56°C) with renowned therapeutic properties. The waters of the nearby **Agnone beach** further to the south, are also healthful, however, they are quite cooler as they spring at 31°C.

Left: another striking shot of the Church of Santa Maria del Soccorso. Right: the splendid Giardino Esotico Gancia.
Below: the long and renowned beach at Citara.

Enormous rocks, worn smooth by the waves and incredibly clear waters once again emphasize the lure the beach of Citara has exerted on visitors for centuries, and make it one of the most popular spots on the island.

A typical view of the splendid greenery surrounding the thermal pools of the Giardini Poseidon.

THE POSEIDON GARDENS

The most important spa complex in the Forio district is known as **Giardini Poseidon**, that overlook the beach of Citara. It was established by Ludwig Kuttner, a Bavarian industrialist with some cooperation from the municipal government. The spa has twenty pools arranged on garden terraces at various heights; they are particularly renowned for the therapeutic properties of their waters that spring from the island's volcanic core.

Near the Citara beach, at Cuotto, there is a fumarole that issues gases at a temperature of 80°C. Further on we see the **Punta Imperatore**, a lavic promontory that offers an incredible view of the entire western part of the island. Then, we can follow a mule trail to the **Faro Imperatore** lighthouse.

PIETRA DI PANZA AND THE "STONE HOUSES"

Another interesting attraction at Forio is **Pietra di Panza**. It is an unusual "building": a tufa block that comprises four dwellings of two or three rooms each and nine cellar rooms for processing grapes. In more general terms, we can say that the so-called "stone houses" are a common type of architecture in several parts of Ischia. Around the II century AD, following a series of cataclysms and earthquakes, enormous blocks of stone came down from Monte Epomeo. The island's residents created shelters for themselves in these stones when they sought refuge from marauding pirates. In some cases they "converted" them into homes, warehouses, cellars and even churches. We can find them at Cuotto, Panza and Ciglio, but the best conserved examples are on the edges of the Falanga forest. They are known as the **Casa Pietro Mosca** and the **Church of Santa Maria del Monte**, situated 401 meters above sea level on a terrace that offers a splendid view of the western part of the island.

The unusual "stone houses", are typical of Ischia's countryside and especially the area of the Falanga forest.

Ischia's Vineyards

Ever since ancient times, the slopes of Ischia's hills have been planted as vineyards that yielded fine red and white wines. These wines, made from the Lacco Ameno, Forio and Ischia vineyards were loaded onto the great sailing ships bound for Rome via Civitavecchia and Genoa. They carried the island's finest product with its unmistakable bouquet to the homes of the wealthiest and most discriminating Italians.

The Sorgeto cove is a combination of wild, natural beauty and enchantment.

SORGETO

Before we reach the tiny village of Sant'Angelo, with its charming little streets and the isthmus that distinguishes the landscape – a landscape that has charmed artists over the decades, we will come upon **Sorgeto**. This little sheltered inlet, that can only be reached by sea, or a very steep staircase is not far from Capo Negro. After many white and sandy beaches, this little cove that barely penetrates the steep rocks, has a wilderness atmosphere, and the most amazingly clear waters.

SERRARA FONTANA

The township of Serrara Fontana, the highest on the Island of Ischia is an attractive grouping of seaside villages, hilly and mountain areas extended from the Marina di Sant'Angelo and Cava Grado to the crest of Monte Epomeo, from Pietra dell'Acqua to the Bocca di Serra point. The two main towns **Fontana** and **Serrara** were originally separate villages inhabited by shepherds and farmers. Fontana is the older of the two, it was mentioned among the island's hamlets as early as 1270, and the place name, *Futane*, carved into a marble panel dated 1370, probably derived from *Fundus*, the Fondo di Sant'Andrea near the hamlet of Noja that is now a part of the township. Serrara was established between the end of the XVI and the beginning of the XVII century; the first written mention of the town is in the document that founded the parish of Santa Maria del Carmine (1641). The church was built in a strategic position near one of the watch towers, at the confluence of four roads that closed off the pass leading to various nearby castles. (In Italian *serrare* means to close or tighten and this could be the root of the town's current name). The two villages were originally part of the parish of Fontana and were ruled by the governor of the island. Later they became part of the *Università del Terzo* and then acquired autonomy in 1806 when with the abolition of feudalism they became a single town. In addition to the two main centers, the town area includes other settlements that are quite far apart, nestled between the sea and Monte Epomeo. One of them is **Ciglio** on the ridge of the mountain, and mentioned in a document dated 1524. Further down is **Succhivo**, the earliest written information about this village dates from the XVI century when it was already part of the jurisdiction of the hamlet of Fontana, or according to other sources, the hamlet of Panza. On the steep Medieval road that led to the Marina di Sant'Angelo is **Iesca**, that may have the "Vigna di Isco" which is mentioned in an XI century document. Near the crest of Monte Epomeo we come to the very old village of **Calimera** from the Greek word *calemera* for "beautiful place." The earliest studies on the thermo-mineral waters of **Cava Scura** date from the fourteenth century; they were known to the Greeks and were already famous during the Roman era. Exploited by the Aragonese, the springs were shown on a map of the Island of Ischia drawn by the famous engraver Mario Cartaro (1586), with the legend *"aqua fervens cavae obscurae."*

The Parish Church of Santa Maria del Carmine and its unmistakable bell-tower-with the archway.

SERRARA

We can reach the center of **Serrara** that is divided into small nuclei because of the configuration of the land itself, by negotiating the curves of the Forio-Ciglio-Serrara-Fontana road that was built between 1884 and 1888.

The main center focuses on *Piazza Pietro Paolo Iacono*, with its large belvedere known as *Punta di Ventaruolo* that offers a magnificent view stretching from Mt. Vesuvius to Punta della Campanella and Capri that is just opposite. The parish church and **Palazzo Iacono** overlook the square. The palazzo, that was built in the XVII century and enlarged in the eighteenth, has a projecting part with mock-ashlar stucco work, topped by a large terrace on the first floor, and a main, rectangular section. Part of the main section is in poor condition, and part has been remodeled so that the upper stories conserve the elegant arrangement of arches with slender pilaster strips that frame the big arched windows. A crenellated tower at the corner of the building still survives.

The seventeenth century **Parish Church of Santa Maria del Carmine** was built on a pass that led to the nearby hamlets; curiously, it is separated from the bell tower by the road. The *façade* has a broken triangular

In the village of Serrara the houses are tightly packed, but here and there we see a little piazza or a church. The entire village overlooks an expanse of bright blue waters.

The splendid hillsides with some of the hamlets that comprise the town of Serrara Fontana that is famous for its thermal-mineral waters. Right: Serrara Fontana's Cava Scura.

tympanum with a circular window. On the right side is the prospect of the lateral nave with the bell tower aedicula, and on the left, beyond the archway that crossed the road, is the three-story bell tower; the first story once connected with the palazzo of the Iacono family that contributed generously to the construction of the church. The *interior* has two naves, with a barrel-vault with lunettes, a transept and large apse against which is the main altar dedicated to Our Lady of Mount Carmel.

Beyond the bell-tower arch, on the state road that leads to Fontana we come to the **Church of the Congregazione dell'Immacolata** in a beautiful setting. This church, with a single nave, and a barrel-vault decorated with lunettes, is flanked by a bell tower with three bells on two levels; it was founded in 1889.

THE FONTANA HILLSIDES

Due to the morphology of the land, **Fontana** which is the highest town on the island, consists of two agglomerates separated by a gorge and linked by the road.

Fontana was the home of the oldest parish church on Ischia. In fact, this church, built by the bishop Bartolomeo de Busulariis of Pavia dates from 1374, as we can see from the stone plaque at the entrance of **Santa Maria la Sacra** today. Originally, the church served defensive purposes, as it was situated in the Fondo of Sant'Andrea, or according to other sources, Santa Maria.

In the early XVI century, another church was built, to replace the original one. This was located in Via Cavumera and was dedicated to Our Lady of the Assumption, it was elevated to the status parish church in 1508, and was named San Sebastiano e Santa Maria la Sacra. This church was destroyed by the earthquake of 1796, and the one we see today was erected in 1885. It is built to a basilica plan with two naves, transept and circular apse.

The heart of the village, however, is the piazza that is dominated by the **Church of Sant'Antonio da Padova**, that dates from the early eighteenth century. Near the square, but set back and in a slightly elevated position, is the **Church of the Immacolata**, an early XVII century structure with a beautiful polychrome marble altar at the rear of the apse. Back in the middle of the piazza, is the *monument to the dead of World Wars I and II*, that was unveiled in 1957. It is from this point that the mule trail begins: it leads to the peak of Monte Epomeo, passing through small chestnut groves and a Mediterranean maquis of great interest to nature enthusiasts.

SANT'ANGELO

The hamlet of **Sant'Angelo** is the seafront community of Serrara Fontana, and also the most famous resort. Its origins are truly ancient: the first settlement dates from the VIII-VII century BC when Greek colonists settled in what is now called **Cava Grado,** a spot that offered a good harbor, a thermal spring and fertile farmland that rose gradually towards Monte Epomeo and was particularly suited to growing grapes and wheat. The archeological finds, mainly geometric and sub-geometric pottery can be dated around VI century, that is when the village disappeared, probably due to natural causes, perhaps crushed by falling alluvial material.

Before the year 1000, Benedictine monks established a small **monastery and small chapel** dedicated to the Archangel Michael on what is known as **Isolotto di Sant'Angelo,** a hump of volcanic land that is connected to the island by a strip of sand. In those days it looked bigger than it does today, and its terraced land was inten-

The old Islet of Sant'Angelo is joined to the Island of Ischia by a long sandbar that stretches opposite the village.

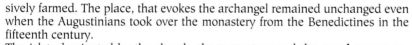
Opposite the islet, between fishing boats and pleasure craft, the village of Sant'Angelo is perched on a tufa ridge in a succession of houses, terraces and hotels.

sively farmed. The place, that evokes the archangel remained unchanged even when the Augustinians took over the monastery from the Benedictines in the fifteenth century.

The islet, dominated by the church, the monastery and the **royal tower** enjoyed a strategic and economic importance until the XVIII century. Then, as the population grew, and following the destruction of the tower and church, under cannon fire from the Bourbon fleet between 1808 and 1809, the people began to move to the other side and this marked the beginning of its decline.

The statue of the saint was transferred to the parish that was built on the Madonnella hill, the **Church of San Michele**, which even today, with its simple, sparkling white façade, bell tower, and tiny cemetery, dominates the village.

Today, the village of Sant'Angelo stretches along the coastal road that goes from Maronti to Cava Grado opposite the islet, which though diminished in size, still connects it with a narrow strip of land, and rises on the ridge of the

tufa rocks where the old fishermen's houses, crowded together, and mostly replaced by pensions and hotels, alternate with terraces and balconies blessed by a breathtaking view. The heart of the village, a famous destination for Italian and international tourists is the *Piazzetta Ottorino Troia*, that opens onto the beach and the little port. Here are luxurious boutiques, shops, restaurants and cafes that are crowded with tourists every evening.

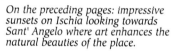

Beyond the hamlet and the old islet of Sant'Angelo, the beautiful Maronti beach, a strip of sand stretches between the lush greenery of the hillside and the deep blue of the sea. The view from Fontana (right) is particularly enchanting, a single glance embraces Testaccio and the Lido dei Maronti.

On the preceding pages: impressive sunsets on Ischia looking towards Sant' Angelo where art enhances the natural beauties of the place.

Views from the hermitage, a holy place that was established on top of Monte Epomeo along with the fifteenth century rock-carved church dedicated to St. Nicholas (right, above).

MONTE EPOMEO

Rising to a height of nearly 800 meters, **Monte Epomeo** is the highest peak on the Island of Ischia, and its orographic fulcrum. Like the other mountains and hills that dot the island, it is not a volcano in the true sense of the term. There is no trace of either a crater or eruptive mouth. Rather it is the result of an underwater eruption, a rise in the earth's crust that occurred during the Quaternary period. The place name is ancient: Strabo and Pliny both emphasized its probable Greek origins: *Epopon* from *exopeus* that means "observe, look around."

A **church** carved out of the tufa, dedicated to St. Nicholas was built on top of Monte Epomeo in the early fifteenth century, and a **hermitage** was built close to three hundred years later. The little church, that was already known as San Nicola di Monte Forte in Casale Fontana in 1504 has a vaulted ceiling, a fine majolica floor, and a marble bas-relief of the saint in pontifical robes. On the left wall there is a chapel with a large reliquary. The cells, carved into the tufa first sheltered pilgrims, and then starting in the mid-seventeenth century, the monks. The hermitage enjoyed its greatest splendor during the latter half of the eighteenth century, and then, starting in the nineteenth it gradually declined.

Vineyards and Wines

The Serrara vineyards, the sloping terraces of Monte Pietra dell'Acqua with beautiful tufa cellars carved into the sides of Mt. Epomeo, or the Pozzale, Croce di Colajanno and Cavalasia vineyards at Succhivo perpetuate one of the island's oldest traditions.

It is here that exceptionally fine wines are made, from the distinctive "Epomeo" to the delightful "Ischia".

BARANO

Barano is located on the south-eastern part of the Island of Ischia, on hillside, just a few kilometers from the sea. It comprises a series of mountains (Cotto, Guardiola, Monte Barano, Monte di Vezzi and Monte di Fiaiano) and a section of coast. Some parts of the coast are very steep and rugged such as "Scarrupata" between Punta San Pancrazio and Capo Grosso, while in others it is flat and sandy, like the Lido dei Maronti that is famous for its fumarole and the radioactive water that comes from the nearby Nitrodi and Olmitello springs. The land presents stratifications of lava flows that date back centuries. It was precisely the eruptions, that occurred in this area for millions of years, especially in the volcanic craters of Testaccio. Vateliero, Molara and Monte Trippodi that made this soil so very fertile.

The toponym, of Latin origin, would seem to derive from the name of a landowner, *Barius* or *Varius*. But ever since antiquity, the various peoples who lived here, including the Siracusans, and of course the Romans, dominated the area, attracted as they were by the fertile land and healthful climate.

During the Middle Ages, however, a terrible tragedy upset the lives the area's inhabitants. On 18 January 1301, an enormous crater opened on the slopes of Monte Trippodi and the lava just poured out. After having devastated the town of Geronda, the incandescent river made its way to the sea where it formed what is known as **Punta Molino**. This tongue of lava (750 meters wide, and 2 kilometers long) later came to be known as *Colata dell'Arso* and today it is covered with a thick pine grove that was planted by the court botanist, Giovanni Gussone, be-

The wild and steep contours of "Scarrupata" between Punta San Pancrazio and Capo Grosso.

Barano in its splendid natural setting.

tween 1853 and 1855. The eruption, that lasted for months, forced the population to seek refuge on the mainland and on the island of Capri. Another dramatic episode in the history of Barano was the invasion by the pirate, Barbarossa Khair ad-Din, the most devastating of the many that plagued the life of Ischia.

Of the three Universitae into which the island was divided during the XVII century, the Città and Isola, Forio, and Terzo, along with Serrara, Fontana and Casamicciola and Lacco, Barano came under the jurisdiction of Terzo. Period documents reveal the hardships these smaller towns suffered during that period, subjected to tithes and other heavy taxes. In 1883 the village was literally ravaged by the violent earthquake that brought all economic development to a halt. In fact, reconstruction focused on the coastal towns; the difficult communications with them made all attempts at recovery particularly difficult for Barano.

THE PARISH CHURCH OF SAN SEBASTIANO MARTIRE

The central piazza is the heart of the village. It is dominated by two religious buildings, the extremely simply church of San Rocco (for whom the piazza itself is named) and the **Parish Church of San Sebastiano Martire** that dates from 1604. It was in that year that the local authorities ordered that Fra Cosmo da Verona build a monastery for Augustinian monks. The monastery, however, was suppressed in 1653 following the bull issued by pope Innocent X that ordered the closing of houses with less than six religious. The parish, however, was created in 1640, when it separated from the parish of San Giorgio. The church has been remodeled many times over the years. Currently the *façade* alternates full and empty spaces surmounted by triangular tympanums. The central part is characterized by a marked vertical sweep emphasized by the single row of pilaster strips that terminates in a denticulate cornice surmounted by another triangular tympanum. The *interior* in the shape of a Latin cross, with four wide arches along the central nave that has a barrel vaulted ceiling decorated with geometric stucco work and lunettes. The apse of the left aisle is illuminated by four very narrow windows in the drum of the small dome. The *bell tower* stands to the left of the church, with its truncated pyramid base it complements the movement created by the façade.

93

TESTACCIO

From a historical standpoint, the most important district of Barano is doubtlessly **Testaccio** which from 1786 to 1873 enjoyed the status of an autonomous municipality. Its importance came from the waters of Succellaro and the stufas of Cacciutto. The **Sudaturo**, today a decrepit building in the heart of the old town was once rather famous. In the eighteenth century, the famous general, Giorgio Corafà, viceroy of Palermo came to live in Testaccio. In 1763, at his own expense, he built the stepped road that leads to the Lido dei Maronti and the Olmitello spring. The town's municipal autonomy as decreed in 1786 led to urban developments that can be seen in Via Giorgio Corafà, the Church of the Assunta and the Parish Church of San Giorgio.

The church of Testaccio, and to the right the steep road that leads down to the Lido dei Maronti.

The eighteenth century **Church of the Assunta** is built to a square plan. The central dome, that has no drum is decorated with stucco work. Today this deconsecrated church is in a state of abandon.

The **Parish Church of San Giorgio** is datable around the end of the XV century. Originally it had a single nave, but then a private oratory was added in 1600 and it was completely remodeled in 1773 when it became known as the **Congregazione di Santa Maria di Costantinopoli**. The left wing of the building dates from 1854. The church is built in the shape of a Latin cross with chapels on the left. On the right, the area that was reserved for the Congregation is longitudinally divided by two pilasters joined by a sturdy arch, and

Lido dei Maronti seen from atop the hills above Testaccio. In the distance, the island of Capri rises from the sea.

The 'Ndrezzata dance"

Among the many picturesque events that are held every year in the town of Barano, the celebrations organized in the district of Buonopane for the feast of St. John the Baptist on the night between 23 and 24 June, and on Easter Monday are truly noteworthy. The "'Ndrezzata (from the Italian word intrecciata for plait) is performed only by residents of Buonopane. They wear typical red, white and green costumes and dance holding a small stick known as the "mazzariello" in their right hand and a wooden sword in the left. The dance, accompanied by music played on wind instruments and a tambourine, ends with a "battle" fought with the swords and the "mazzariello."

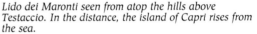

the domical vaults are decorated with stucco work. Next to the church there is a bell tower with two cornices that continue from the façade without any break.

Along an alleyway that leads to the Sudaturo, we come to the **Church of Santa Maria delle Grazie**, where the Congregation of the parish church of San Giorgio moved during the first half of the twentieth century. This rectangular church, with a curved apse was built in 1748; the *interior* is graced by complex decorations.

Near San Giorgio there is a XV century **tower**. Used mainly as a lookout point and defensive structure, it later became the home of the local baron. Square, without any base, the tower now stands abandoned, its two stories seem to be decorated with piperino corbels.

Fiaiano, that is located in the middle of the area where the terrible eruption of 1301 began, is characterized by a thick pine grove. Here we find the small seventeenth century **Parish Church of Sant'Anna**, and the **Church of the Madonna delle Grazie** that was built in the mid-eighteenth century.

THE ISLAND OF PROCIDA

The smallest of the Phlegraean islands is located off the coast of Capo Miseno, across the Procida Channel, just a short distance from Ischia. Along with Ischia, and the small sickle shaped island of Vivara, **Procida** is one of the most obvious manifestations of the volcanic activity of the nearby Phlegraean Fields. Procida itself is the result of ancient underwater eruptions, that are common to the Phlegraean area, and this is demonstrated by the composition of its rocks that consist of tufa, trachyte and basalt formations. Even the shape of the coastline, with its many outcroppings is proof of its volcanic origin as the contours of at least five crater edges can be discerned.

Inhabited since the earliest prehistoric times, the island was colonized by the Greeks who called it *Pròchyta*. In the XIII century it was a fief of the Da Procida, the noble family that gave the island its name. Giovanni was the most famous of its sons. If it shared the vicissitudes of nearby Ischia until the end of the XVIII century, in the following years Procida would be occupied by the English in an anti-French mode. The island's landscape is picturesque, and quite awe-inspiring: from the splendid sandy shores that reach to the deep azure waters, to the romantic Punta di Solchiaro and Punta Pioppeto, where the eye can feast on enchanting vistas, to the colorful center of Procida. Here the lively colors of the houses, are typically Mediterranean with arches as the main element of an almost oriental style of architecture. Terraces, domes and narrow alleys and underpasses: everything in Procida contributes to painting a unique picture. The noteworthy highlights include the old district of **Terra Murata** with the **Church of San Michele** that was part of an abbey, with a fine coffered ceiling and a painting of *Saint Michael Defeating Lucifer* by Luca Giordano (XVII century). Not far from the *Marina di Sancio Cattolico*, the main harbor of Procida is the **Sanctuary of Santa Maria delle Grazie.** The building is surmounted by a high dome that rests on a polygonal drum. Inside are the tombs of the twelve martyrs of Procida (1799).

Two views of the small, picturesque Island of Procida that is dominated by the massive castle

Every year the ritual procession winds its way through the streets of Procida.

POZZUOLI

A rather sizable town, **Pozzuoli** overlooks the central portion of the gulf of the same name, that is bounded by Capo Miseno and the island of Nisida, in an extremely picturesque setting. A popular spa and beach resort, with thriving industries and businesses, Pozzuoli is the main port of departure for the Phlegraean islands. It is also a major point of interest as regards archeology, the arts and geology. It is situated in the Phlegraean Fields district, in an area that is still volcanically active. The land is highly subject to bradyseismic shifts and telluric phenomena. It was established as a colony of Samo in the middle of the VI century BC and was originally called *Dikaiarchia*. It allied itself with Cumae and faced the Etruscans and then the Sannites who conquered it in the V century BC. In the II century BC it was Romanized and renamed *Puteoli*. The town became famous as a port, and in all likelihood was the main strategic base for the Roman fleet in the Mediterranean, at least until the founding of the port of Ostia (I century AD). Notwithstanding the decline brought about by this event, it was highly respected by the emperors, and specifically Domitian who linked it to the imperial capital via the road that bore his name. St. Paul visited Pozzuoli and wrote about it in the *Acts of the Apostles*; the city suffered through repeated barbarian invasions and with the fall of the empire (V-VI century AD) it lost the protection it enjoyed from Rome. The barbarians along with the changed dynamics of the land itself caused by the intensive bradyseismic phenomena caused the population to emigrate to Naples and other, safer places. Contemporaneously, the inexorable sinking of the original harbor's infrastructures led to its being transformed into a fishing town, while at the same time the activities linked to the area's hot springs were favored and incentivated. Recently, the increase in the bradyseismic and geological shifts has led to the evacuation of some parts of the historical center, revealing the precarious existence of the settlements in the Phlegraean area.

At Pozzuoli what is called the Temple of Serapis (on these pages) was actually a public market in Roman times.

Views of the impressive ruins of the Flavian Amphitheater at Pozzuoli.

THE TEMPLE OF SERAPIS

Also known as *Serapeo*, this is certainly one of the most monumental traces of the Roman era in the lower portion of the town. It has even yielded up the vestiges of a *wharf* from the Augustan era. Although it owes its name to the discovery of a statue of *Serapis*, an ancient Egyptian divinity worshipped during the Hellenistic and Roman era, the impressive ruins we admire today are actually those of a large public market. The *Macellum* that was originally the place were foodstuffs, mainly meats and fish, were sold, occupies a quadrangle bounded by porticoes that housed the shops that could also be entered from the outside. On the side facing the main entrance there was an apse with niches where statues once stood. The central portion of the courtyard contained a round podium with a central fountain that was also decorated with statues.

A group of sixteen African marble columns with Corinthian capitals supported the trabeation that was originally topped by a dome. These structures date mainly from the Flavian period, but restorations and remodeling became necessary following seismic events that occurred in the I century AD and later periods (II-III centuries). Today, the great interest in what is known as the **Temple of Serapis**, is due to some features that make it possible to understand the dynamics of the bradyseismic events in the district at a glance – naturally in addition to its outstanding architectural and archeological value. These impressive ruins are partly submerged by sea and thermo-mineral waters that have overflowed as the ground level has lowered. On the remains of the columns that stand, mutilated, on the circular podium and on the three of the four large ones that once fronted the apse room that opened onto the portico, we can see the holes produced by date mussels, a species of mollusk that perforates the stones they attach themselves to, so that we now have a clear visual map of the changes in the water level due to bradyseismic phenomena.

The Flavian Amphitheater and the underground chambers.

THE FLAVIAN AMPHITHEATER

The upper section of the town, in an area that has revealed traces of other structures from the Roman period, such as the **smaller amphitheater** (*opus incertum* ruins of a structure built during the reign of Augustus) and the **Cardito Pool** (a system of communicating pools), also include the significant ruins of the **Flavian Amphitheater**. It was completed during the realm of the emperor Vespasian in the second half of the I century AD and therefore is younger than the smaller amphitheater. The Flavian Amphitheater is the third largest in Italy after the Coliseum in Rome and the amphitheater of Santa Maria Capua Vetere. This outstanding example of the skill of Roman builders owes its excellent state of conservation – and especially the underground rooms – to the enormous amounts of volcanic ash and debris that have been deposited over the centuries due to the eruptions of the nearby Solfatara. The first archaeological assays, along with the first excavations were undertaken during the first

Still more pictures of the fascinating underground chambers of the Flavian Amphitheater.

half of the last century, but it was only in the late 'forties that it was possible to bring to light what remains of its original might that had been hidden for centuries under enormous quantities of debris. On the outside, the amphitheater originally had three orders of arches crowned by an attic. Inside, we can see the elliptical "field" that measures 75 x42 meters. It is cut transversally by a corridor covered by grates that correspond to the many hatches in the floor of the arena, that were used during the spectacles. The *tiers* that comprised the cavea were originally arranged in three orders only two of which have survived, but on the whole they are quite well preserved. The amphitheater could accommodate an audience of 40,000. A large number of portals that we can still see on the tiers, regulated access; through a series of steps the spectators could reach the various sections of the tiers that were divided by a series of still visible wedges.

The outstanding point of archeological interest, that allows us to understand how the games and spectacles were presented, is without a doubt the **underground chambers**. They consist of one corridor beneath the ellipse that follows its contours, and two orthogonally intersecting corridors. These structures, built mainly of brick were completed between the I and II century AD and have reached us in an excellent state of conservation. In fact, they provide an excellent understanding of how the circuses and gladiatorial battles against ferocious beasts were organized. Today we know for certain that the many quadrangular hatches, equipped with complex systems of pulleys and ropes, in the floor were used to raise the cages with the wild animals that were then released into the arena. In addition to providing fresh air to the underground chambers, the hatches were also used to bring the materials needed for the games and spectacles into the arena. It has also been proved that a complex plumbing system brought water from the aqueduct into the arena so that it could be flooded for mock naval battles (*naumachiae*). During the second half of the XVII century, with the reconstruction of a portion of the underground chambers, attempts were made to dig up the **Chapel of Saint Gennaro**, in tribute to a deeply rooted tradition according to which the future patron saint of Naples was exposed, along with other followers, to the fury of the beasts but was spared.

Solfatara, the landscape is desolate and lunar.

THE SOLFATARA

Just outside the inhabited section, a branch of the Via Domiziana will lead us to the **Solfatara** one of the most tangible examples of secondary volcanic phenomena in the Phlegraean Fields. Already known to the Romans as *Forum Vulcani* it consists of a the large crater of an old volcano that is currently in a dormant phase (the last eruption occurred during the XII century). This phase, that is also known as "solfatara" of the volcanic system near Pozzuoli is typical of post-volcanic activity since the only thing the volcano "does" is to emit sulfurous gases that create sulfur deposits as a result of condensation.

A visit to the Solfatara, that is only possible with an escort of expert guides, is as interesting as it is unforgettable. The barren, desert landscape seems unreal; it is enlivened only by the hot steam (around 100°C), spurts of hot mud, the carbon dioxide (*mofete*) and mineral water springs. The crater is elliptical in shape, and its walls consist of tufa and trachyte rock. The only masonry structures in the Solfatara are those of the old **Observatory** situated near the Large Mouth and those of the **Stufe** were fumaroles spout at temperatures of around 100°C. One typical phenomenon we can observe inside the Solfatara is the condensation of water vapor that resembles a small cloud near a free flame.

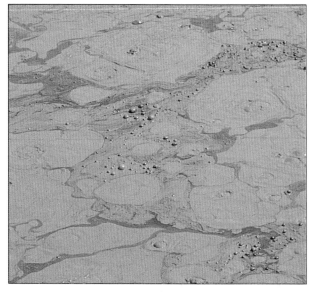

Different views of the Solfatara and clear signs of its volcanic origins.

BACOLI-CAPO MISENO

For those coming from Baia, along the picturesque road that dominates the western part of the Gulf of Pozzuoli, the first sign of **Bacoli** is the imposing square structure of the **Castle of Baia** that was built by Don Pedro of Toledo, viceroy of Spain in the XVI century to protect the coastal settlements from pirate raids. Bacoli is a small town known for its fishing business and lovely resorts. It was founded by the Greeks and quickly became a favorite of the Romans who built villas and houses that are clear evidence of the Roman *Bauli*. The **Hundred Chambers**, in particular, arranged on two levels were a complex mechanism that supplied water to one of the area's villas. The lower, and older, level consists of a network of conduits that lead into the sea; the upper level holds a large I century AD cistern. The **Piscina Mirabile** is a formidable water reservoir that was used by the Roman fleet when it docked at Capo Miseno. Known as the largest cistern of ancient times, it was built during the reign of the emperor Augustus. Near the beach there are yet other ruins that are incorrectly known as the **tomb of Agrippina**. Actually, these ruins have nothing to do with Nero's mother who was killed under orders from her son and buried at Bauli. They are merely visible evidence of a small theater that stood adjacent to a large Roman villa that overlooked the sea.

Capo Miseno, the remains of an ancient volcano corroded by the sea, dominates an unusual landscape marked by craters (Lago Miseno and Porto di Miseno) that document the volcanic nature of this maritime appendage to the Phlegraean Fields. Its shape, that recalls the tumulus type tombs fueled the ancient legend that this was the burial place of mythical heroes. Its slopes are scattered with Roman ruins that include what may have been a villa that belonged to Marius Gaius. During the Augustan era Miseno was the main Tyrrhenian port of the Roman navy, and this was the basis for the rise of today's fishing village of the same name.

A panorama of Bacoli and Capo Miseno with the distinctive outlines of Capri in the background.

A panorama of Bacoli and Capo Miseno with the distinctive outlines of Capri in the background.

BAIA

Today part of the municipality of Bacoli, **Baia** is a seaside resort in a picturesque setting overlooking the gulf that gives it its name. The place, however, is famous for an enormous **archeological area** that has given us exceptional ruins and evidence of the Roman civilization in the westernmost portion of the Gulf of Naples.

The fortunes of Roman *Baiae* began during the late Republican period. At that time, the abundance of curative spring waters, along with particularly inviting climate prompted Romans to settle here on a permanent basis. They built numerous beautiful houses and patrician villas in the enchanting scenario of Baia. The place has been celebrated by Latin writers and poets. If the words of Horace, Livy, Martial and Statius alone are sufficient testimony of the beauties of the place, the villas that belonged to some of the most famous members of the Roman political and social order prove that Baia was a favored residence that could not be easily matched elsewhere. During the imperial era it was the exclusive residence of the emperors who also bought up the private homes conferring an imprint of magnificence and lavishness upon a place which, like Capri, soon became a jewel of the empire. Thus, Baia became the witness and theater of some significant events in the tortured history of Rome under the Caesars, as well as ambitious projects and manifestations of eccentric folly.

Later, the unarrestable sequences of accentuated bradyseismic submersion, along with the disastrous effects of repeated eruptions of the Phlegraean volcanoes led to the nearly total disappearance of the Roman settlement and its grandeur. Only after World War II have painstaking excavations made it possible to bring to light some major vestiges of ancient *Baiae*.

Two pictures of the Theater-Nymphaeum with the circular pool in archeological area of Baia.

Buildings and rooms that were probably part of the baths in ancient Baia.

THE ARCHEOLOGICAL AREA

The impressive ruins that have been brought to light, scattered along the broad terraced slope that extends from the top of the hill, were probably part of the ancient imperial *Palatium* complex and reveal structures of which only a minimal part were dedicated to baths and springs. The buildings date back to the period ranging from the I to IV century AD. The ruins, that are connected by ramps, steps and corridors are "divided" into the sectors named Sosandra, Mercury and Venus. The **Sosandra sector** that gets its name from a marble statue found in an inside room, presents the ruins of an elegant home and a **Theater-Nymphaeum** with a circular pool. A large lower terrace contains the ruins of what is known as **Sosandra's Bath**, a pool with a loggia that drew its water from a thermal spring that is still active. The **Mercury sector**, that was erroneously believed to have been a temple, consists of a round building that was most probably used for baths; its *opus reticulatum* walls support the spherical vault. The **Venus sector**, is arranged

The Temple of Venus and on the left, the ruins of the Temple of Diana.

on various levels along the terraced slopes and comprises several rooms one of which housed an Exedra-Nymphaeum that was complete with a fountain. The **Temples of Venus** and **Diana** complete the panorama of architectural ruins at Baia. The temple of Venus, that was probably connected to the sector named for the goddess is built in the typical octagonal shape with large windows. The doorway is flanked by niches that also embellish the building's outer perimeter. The interior, that is circular, is open to the sky as the original ceiling has collapsed to the ground. The **Temple of Diana** is situated outside the archeological area proper, not too far from the Cumae railroad station. This building has marked structural and architectural similarities with the Temple of Venus, both in its shape and plan. The spherical dome that once covered it is only partly extant, and this gives it a very unusual appearance.

CUMA

The archeological area of Cuma is one of the most important in the region. It extends south of the reclaimed plain of Licola, on the hills between the Tyrrhenian Sea and the Lake of Averno. This was site of one of the most advanced Greek cities in all southern Italy. The Chalcidians from Eubea settled in these places (VIII century BC) that were certainly inhabited in prehistoric times and, according to some sources, were the outposts of colonists from AEolia as early as the XI century BC. The power of the Cumaean state rose to such an extent that in a short time it dominated the entire surrounding area, from Miseno to *Puteoli*, and laid the basis for the founding of *Neapolis*. Threatened by the Etruscan and other Italic peoples that did not tolerate its power, Cuma won decisive victories in the VI and V centuries BC; the last of these marked the definitive collapse of Etruscan expansion in Magna Grecia. Overcome by the Sannites (second half of the V century BC) and then Romanized, it offered concrete support to its powerful neighbor during the Punic Wars so that it became a *Municipium*. Its sad destiny began during the Middle Ages, and was sealed after it was razed to the ground by Saracen pirates (X century).

Cuma: the Temple of Apollo.

Following pages: the Temple of Apollo and a detail of the Via Sacra.

Cuma, a panorama looking towards the baths and the Temple of the Capitoline Triad.

The Temple of Jupiter seen from two different angles.

THE ARCHEOLOGICAL AREA

The archeological vestiges of Cuma that include the ruins of many temples, public and private buildings, the acropolis and a vast cemetery are located in an area that stretches from the pine grove of Licola to what is known as the **Arch of Felix**, a building with a single archway that dates from the I century, and the reign of Domitian. Nearby is the **Grotto of Cocceio** which was an underground passage that linked the city to the Lake of Averno. Further on the road forks, one side leads to the meager vestiges of the I century BC **Amphitheater**, and the other to the large **necropolis** that has yielded up traces of Roman tombs from the republican and imperial eras, as well as very old graves that can be dated between the IX and VII centuries BC and that bear astounding similarities to Mycenaean funerary architecture.

After we pass the **Tomb of the Sibyl**, we come to the **Forum**. This large, and partly porticoed area comprises the Temple of the Capitoline Triad and the **Baths** that were built between the I and II century AD. The **Temple of the Capitoline Triad**, originated in the IV century BC and was extensively rebuilt during the imperial period. The building has given considerable fragments of sculptures of the gods that once adorned it. The **Acropolis** bears distinctive traces of Greek fortifications (V century BC), that were strengthened by the Romans who wanted to improve the defenses of a place that was already quite inaccessible due to the barrenness of the land. We reach the acropolis by going along the *Via Sacra*, a road built from large slabs of volcanic rock. On the right we can admire the ruins of the **Temple of Apollo**, a Greek building

The Temple of Jupiter and the baptismal font. On the left, the acropolis.

Below, the Cumaean archeological area near the Sibyl's Cave.

that was remodeled during the both the Sannite and Roman periods. Originally peripteral it presents the ruins of columns and bases that are the signs of work done during the Augustan era. Between the VI and VII centuries it was converted from a pagan temple into a Christian basilica, and some of the tombs and baptismal fonts date from that period.

On the acropolis esplanade, in a site that offers a breathtaking panorama, stands the **Temple of Jupiter** that bears several structural similarities to the temple of Apollo. Built by the Greeks (V century BC) it was completely transformed under Augustus. The work has made it totally impossible to see the oldest parts of the building that was later converted into a Christian basilica (V-VI century). There are the well preserved ruins of a circular baptismal font, bits of *opus reticulatum* walls and vestiges of Christian tombs.

One of the most famous elements in the entire archeological area of Cuma is the **Cave of the Cumaean Sibyl**. It was one of the most popular sanctuaries of the ancient world, it was carved into the tufa rock by the Greeks (VI-V century BC). It is trapezoidal and extends over one hundred meters in length. It is quite well preserved, except for the first section that is open to the sky, and it shows signs of having been restructured in later years (IV-III century BC). Here we can admire a marble epigraph with verses from Virgil's Aeneid, some cisterns and a rectangular room with a niche that is believed to be the place where the Sybil made her prophecies. Not far from this tunnel is the entrance to the **Roman Crypt**, a large cavity beneath Mount Cuma and that had a function similar to that of the Grotto of Cocceio.

Two different views of the Sibyl's Cave.

With its little port the village of
Forio is nestled against the slopes
of Monte Epomeo. ◆ 53

Casamicciola today, is welco
and luxuriantly green. ◆ 35

The picturesque, closely
crowded white houses of
Lacco Ameno. ◆ 39

Rising to nearly 800 meters,
Monte Epomeo is the highest
mountain on the Island of
Ischia.
◆ 90

Ischia Porto sn
has long been a
◆ 23

The Giardini Poseidon. ◆ 73

The Mushroom. ◆ 46

The long and famous
sandy beach at Citara.
◆ 69

Baia di
S. Montano

116
M. Vico

Il Fungo

Lacco
Ameno

Casamicciola

Spiaggia
degli Inglesi

Ischia P

S. Restituta

Spiaggia di
S. Francesco

S. Alessandro

Punta del
Soccorso

Forio

ISOLA D'ISCHIA

M. Epomeo
788

M. Trippodi
503

Fiaiano

Giardini
Poseidon

Fontana

Spiaggia
di Citara

Piedimonte

Campagr

Punta
Imperatore

Buonopane

Serrara
Fontana

Barano
d'Ischia

Chiumanno

Scarrupata

The picturesque village
of Serrara.
◆ 77

Panza

Testaccio

Succhivo

S. Angelo

Sorgeto

Fumarole
Giardini
Aphrodite

Marina
dei Maronti

Sant'Angelo, an unmistakable
islet and village.
◆ 82

Cuma, the Temple of Jupiter.
◆ 119

The Theater-Nymphaeum and the circular pool in the archeological area at Baia.
◆ 115

...ral cove ...ular port.

CUMA

L. d'Averno

L. di Fusaro

Lido di Napoli

Golfo di Pozzuoli

Baia

Pozzuoli

Torregaveta

Cappella

Bacoli

Acquamorta

Miseno

Capo Miseno

Pozzuoli, the Temple of Serapis.
◆ 101

Canale di procida

Capo Bove

Procida

Lido di Procida

ISOLA VIVARA

ISOLA DI PROCIDA

A view of Bacoli and Capo Miseno against the incomparable backdrop of Capri rising from the sea. ◆ 112

Procida is dominated by the mighty castle.
◆ 99

Just off the coast of Ischia, the islet with the impressive Aragonese castle.
◆ 8

...rano, in a splendid natural ...tting.
92

TYRRHENIAN SEA

INDEX